Charting the Course
Special Education in Charter Schools

Azure D. S. Angelov

David F. Bateman

Council for Exceptional Children
2900 Crystal Drive, Suite 1000
Arlington, VA 22202

www.cec.sped.org

The Chapter 1 section "Special Education Statutes and Concepts" is adapted with permission from Improving Access and Creating Exceptional Opportunities for Students with Disabilities in Public Charter Schools, by L. M. Rhim & P. T. O'Neill. Copyright 2013 by the National Alliance for Public Charter Schools.

Library of Congress Cataloging-in-Publication data

Angelov, Azure.
Charting the course: Special education in charter schools / by Azure D. S. Angelov and David F. Bateman.
p. cm.
Includes biographical references.

ISBN 978-0-86586-515-0 (soft cover edition)
ISBN 978-0-86586-516-7 (eBook edition)

Design by Devall Advertising.

Printed in the United States of America by United Graphics LLC.

First edition 10 9 8 7 6 5 4 3 2 1

Contents

Contributors

Parker Baxter
Director of Knowledge
National Association of Charter School Authorizers

Scott Bess
President and Chief Operating Officer
Goodwill Education Initiatives

Brandon Brown
Senior Vice President
The Mind Trust

Kristin Hines
Senior Director of School Incubation
The Mind Trust

Kim Hymes
Associate Director of Federal Relations
National Center for Learning Disabilities

Karega Rausch
Vice President of Research and Evaluation
National Association of Charter School Authorizers

Lauren Morando Rhim
Co-Founder and Executive Director
National Center of Special Education in Charter Schools

Christy Wolfe
Senior Policy Advisor
National Alliance of Public Charter Schools

Acknowledgments

Two primary communities have informed this work: the field of special education and the charter school sector. Several professional organizations and influential individuals have come together to make this book possible. We would like to thank the Council for Exceptional Children, the National Association of Charter School Authorizers, the National Alliance of Public Charter Schools, the National Center for Special Education in Charter Schools, the National Center on Learning Disabilities, The Mind Trust, and the National Association of State Directors of Special Education for their ongoing support of this work.

We also thank our chapter contributors Lauren Morando Rhim, Parker Baxter, Christy Wolfe, Kim Hymes, Scott Bess, Karega Rausch, Kristin Hines, and Brandon Brown. Our case study participants' inspirational work continues to be relentless in the name of all students, and so we are also grateful to Tonya Taylor and Laura Cope, Goodwill Education Initiatives; Karen Caruso, Lola Software; Caitlin Teague and Carey Dahncke, Christel House; Nancy Opalack and Beth Giovannetti, Education Support Systems; Naomi Rubin DeVeaux, District of Columbia Public Charter School Board; Dixon Deutsch, New York City Charter School Center; Caprice Young and Kelly Hourigan, Magnolia Public Charter Schools, together with Sydney Quon, Los Angeles Unified School District.

We'd also like to thank the members of the Council for Exceptional Children for all their efforts toward improving services for students with disabilities and their families. For their assistance on this book, we would like to acknowledge CEC's Publications Manager, Lorraine Sobson; our copyeditor, Elizabeth Ferry Slocum; and our proofreader, Deborah Whitley, for their impressive attention to detail and excellent work.

Finally, special thanks to Eileen Ahearn for her tireless efforts to be at the forefront of both charter schools and special education.

Foreword

It is a pleasure for me to comment on this important new book focused on charter schools and special education. As the opening sections describe, special education grew as a field from early assistance for struggling students in the 19th century to the extensive set of laws and regulations that now require every public school to meet the needs of students with disabilities. In 1991, charter schools came on the scene and, as public schools, also had to adhere to those requirements.

This book's five chapters, seven case studies, numerous charts, and appendices are highly informative. The topics covered include information about early charter leaders such as Albert Shanker and Ray Budde, as well as discussions about special education funding, programming, and administration of special education in the charter setting; start-up and close-down of charter schools; and the importance of individual education programs (IEPs) and Section 504 plans.

Charter schools are a part of the American public education system. Their contributions to the field of education as well as the problems that trouble them are important and need to be acknowledged and addressed. This book contributes to an understanding of the field and discusses the important work related to special education that must continue to support success in both charter and traditional schools throughout the United States.

Eileen Ahearn
Project Director
National Association of State Directors of Special Education

CHAPTER 1

Charter Schools and Special Education

With Lauren Morando Rhim

Since the early 1990's, charter schools have sought to provide a public school choice option for parents and students in communities across the country. Although still a publically funded school, charter schools have distinct characteristics which differ from traditional public schools, namely exemption from certain state/local rules and regulations in exchange for increased accountability requirements.

Over the last two decades, 40 states and the District of Columbia have passed charter school laws. Charter schools are now serving two million students in 5,500 schools, nationwide.

As public schools, charter schools must comply with all federal education laws, including the Individuals with Disabilities Education Act (IDEA) and the Elementary and Secondary Education Act (ESEA). Despite this requirement, there have been reports that students with disabilities are underrepresented in charter schools. While the reasons for this under enrollment are debatable, some reports have indicated that charter schools do not have the capacity to identify, evaluate, and serve students with disabilities, particularly students with significant disabilities.

CEC believes that charter schools must reflect a commitment to free and universal public education, with equality and educational opportunity for all. As such, charter schools, the chartering agency and authorizer, and ultimately the highest governmental authority, must ensure that the rights of children and youth with exceptionalities are upheld.

Council for Exceptional Children, 2015

Public education in the United States was originally established as part of the Department of War in the early 19th century, when it became apparent that the United States could not sustain an effective military with large numbers of illiterate soldiers (p. ix, Cross, 2004). Over the years, public education grew in size and mission, reflecting the changes in the nation.

With the *Brown v. Board of Education* Supreme Court decision in 1954, public education entered a new era that prioritized equal access to public education for all students, especially those who had been marginalized in the system of racially segregated schools. Although the *Brown* decision dealt with segregation by race, it established an important legal concept that separate education facilities are inherently unequal, thereby setting the stage for contemporary civil rights advocacy in public education.

The second half of the 20th century was a time of emerging ideas in the field of education. Research efforts advancing understanding of the demographic makeup and needs of the students whom public education was trying to serve (and not serve) began to gain more traction, along with emerging theories and ideas focused on restructuring and redesigning public education. In 1965, President Lyndon B. Johnson signed the Elementary and Secondary Education Act into law, sharing his belief that "full educational opportunity [should be] our first national goal"(Peters & Woolley, 2016). Educators from various walks of life were beginning to look at public education more critically, with intentions of improving the system as a whole. The Education for All Handicapped Children Act, in 1975, was the first law to stipulate that students should receive a free and appropriate public education, regardless of ability. The Council for Exceptional Children (CEC), a known voice in special education since its founding in 1922, provided crucial support in the passage of this groundbreaking legislation. But it was not until 1983, when the National Commission on Excellence in Education released *A Nation at Risk*, that educational reform became part of the mainstream dialogue.

Ray Budde, in *Education by Charter* (1988, although he first presented the concept a decade earlier to the Society for General Systems Research), recommended a restructuring of public school systems by allowing groups of teachers to start autonomous "charter schools" within existing districts, hence a decentralized model of public education. Since that time, charter schools and special education have each been both a driving force in public school reform efforts and a catalyst for advocacy of high-quality public educational experiences for students, teachers, and schools. Whereas fundamental special education laws have been passed establishing the civil rights of people with disabilities, the charter movement has focused on a form of governance designed to improve schools for students and teachers. Knowing some of the history of both provides both insight into the spirit and intent of each, and clues as to how to bring them together for a more promising future.

Key Actors in Education Reform

Elizabeth Farrell, Early Special Education Advocate

There is simply no way to discuss the evolution of special education without acknowledging Elizabeth Farrell. Farrell received a teaching degree from Oswego Normal and Training School (now the State University of New York at Oswego) in 1895; she went on to study teaching, specifically Johann Heinrich Pestalozzi's philosophies of education, for 2 more years. Pestalozzi was an 18th century Swiss educational reformist whose methods and philosophies became known as the Pestalozzi method. His teachings advocated for educating the whole child, reforming school for the poor, and inclusion. Pestalozzi's work would not only influence Elizabeth Farrell but it would also be foundational to her career.

In 1899, Farrell became the teacher of her first "ungraded" class in the New York City public school system. The class had 19 students, 12 of whom were deemed "retarded," ranging in age from 8 to 16. By 1903, the New York City public schools had opened 10 ungraded classes modeled after Farrell's. In 1906, she became Inspector of the Ungraded Class Department for the New York City Department of Education and under her leadership, the department navigated a significant level of growth. By 1911 there were more than 130 ungraded classrooms. In 1913 she opened a diagnostic clinic that included psychology, social services, education, and medical departments. A story about her in *The New York Times* (Editorial, 1913) focused on the cooperation necessary among schools, courts, hospitals, prisons, and immigration authorities to support the education of students with "mental defects."

> **A story about Elizabeth Farrell in *The New York Times* (Editorial, 1913) focused on the cooperation necessary among schools, courts, hospitals, prisons, and immigration authorities to support the education of students with "mental defects."**

In 1915, Farrell founded the scholarly journal *Ungraded*, which was published by the Ungraded Teachers Association of New York City until 1926. She taught coursework for future ungraded teachers at the University of Pennsylvania; the School of Pedagogy at New York University; and Teachers College, Columbia University. In 1922, Farrell continued her advocacy of students with exceptionalities by founding the International Council of Exceptional Children and serving as its president until 1926.

••

Case Study: The Era of Educational Innovation

Los Angeles Unified School District
Los Angeles, California

Karen Caruso is a National Board Certified Teacher with master's degrees in both psychology and education. She has been a teacher in the Los Angeles Unified School District (LAUSD) for 20 years. In her spare time away from her third-grade classroom, she teaches future teachers at the University of California, Los Angeles, Graduate School of Education. In 2010, Caruso and some of her colleagues were unwittingly thrust into the public eye when the *Los Angeles Times* ran a story, "Who's Teaching L.A.'s Kids?" (Felch, Song, & Smith), scrutinizing their practice based on value-added measures, student test scores, and other predictive data. Caruso recalled feeling that she "was at Ground Zero in an assault on teachers. My name was in the public. Reporters were calling my students' parents. I was completely blindsided."

A couple of years later, Caruso was working with a student named Lola, who had been born premature and had a variety of challenges. "Lola was an amazing little girl, but if I gave her more than one direction at a time, she was completely lost. I tried Post-it Notes on her desk, and her mom did the same thing at home, but they were difficult to revise, they got lost and crumpled." Caruso herself has a hearing loss—"No matter how hard I try, I can't make my ears work better"—and has benefited from technology. Could Lola's executive function skills be improved with the help of technology? From this experience, Lola Software was born (http://www.lolatechsystems.com).

LAUSD is home to more than 270 charter schools, with a collective enrollment of more than 135,000 students. "The charters in LAUSD were so enthusiastic about using Lola," Caruso said. "They were really open to trying new things and implementing new ideas. Education is supposed to evolve. Technology can scaffold instruction in a whole new way. Ed tech should start with teachers. Teachers have the ideas and innovation to take our profession back. I feel like we've lived through the dark ages and are moving into an era of innovation in education."

How does a teacher with an innovative idea for helping students make the dream a reality? As Lola moves into beta testing, Caruso offered the following pieces of advice for other educators who believe they have a game-changing idea:

- There is no flight plan to go from teacher to tech start-up. You have to be willing to figure it out and make it happen.

- There are lots of layers and steps, including your school bureaucracy, tech development, investors, and a legal team.

- If your idea is driven by your students, keep them as your focus. Students should be your North Star.

- You have to make the conscious decision that failure is not an option. When you hit an obstacle, you have to keep moving forward. Don't accept no as an answer; don't give up if you think it will help more students.

- Collaborate, collaborate, collaborate, collaborate.

- Find partners who believe in you and your mission.

Ray Budde and "Education by Charter"

As noted previously, Ray Budde is credited with developing the initial concept of charter schools. Budde served in the Navy during World War II; he earned his bachelor's degree from St. Louis University, a master's degree in business administration from the University of Illinois, and then a doctorate in education from the University of Michigan. His work as a seventh-grade English teacher and assistant principal in Lansing, Michigan, provided him with on-the-ground experiences in public education early in his career. He went on to accept a faculty position at the University of Massachusetts Amherst, where he became interested in organizational theory.

Budde's *Education by Charter: Restructuring School Districts* (1988) captured the attention of educators and policy makers. In later pieces Budde delved into policy aspects of restructuring education (1995) and also shared his perspective on many aspects of the charter movement (1996). In "The Evolution of the Charter Concept," he described the evolution of his idea from its conceptualization in 1974 through the 1988 publication:

> Even though there was considerable dissatisfaction with the public schools, no one felt that things were so bad that the system itself needed to be changed. Innovation was the theme of the times, and innovation could take place within the present system. Find some new idea or program, and then all that was needed was some in-service training and presto: education in your school would be improved! With all the studies and reports of the 1980s, I decided to take another look at the concept and try again. (Budde, 1996, p. 72)

For the final 12 years of his professional life, Budde served as executive director for the Blackstone Valley Educational Collaborative, an organization supporting school districts in Massachusetts.

Albert Shanker, the Tough Liberal

By all accounts, Albert Shanker had a truly amazing professional journey. He was very different from Budde in his experiences, approaches, and rationale for reforming public education via charter schools. Born to Jewish-Russian immigrant parents, Shanker did not speak English when he entered first grade in the New York City public schools. His public education experience—both as a student and, later, as a teacher in East Harlem—would become not only the foundation for his impressive oratory skills but also part of his professional motivation. From 1964 to 1986, Shanker served as president of the United Federation of Teachers union (later to become the American Federation of Teachers) in New York City. In this role he navigated strikes, mergers, and negotiations, gaining critics and supporters alike. He walked with Martin Luther King, Jr., in Selma, Alabama; secured the pensions and retirement funds of New York public school teachers; organized paraprofessionals in 1960; and created the first ever "career ladder" program for paraprofessional recruitment into teaching. He advised President Jimmy Carter; embraced the *Nation at Risk* report (National Commission on Excellence in Education, 1983); and posthumously received the Presidential Medal of Freedom in 1998. In presenting this medal, President Bill Clinton said

> Albert Shanker illuminated our Nation's path toward educating our children with devastating honesty, sharp wit, and profound wisdom. He was one of the most important teachers of the 20th century. In 1983, when the *Nation At Risk* report challenged us to do far more to raise educational standards for all our children, Al Shanker was one of the very first to answer the call. (Clinton, 1998)

Shanker was an early supporter of charter schools. In 1988 he publicly supported Budde's charter school concept as a way to reform school districts systematically, encouraging teachers to open autonomous schools in existing school buildings:

> Do not think of a school as a building, and you can see how it works. Consider six or seven or twelve teachers in a school who say, "We've got an idea. We've got a way of doing something very different. We've got a way of reaching the kids that are now not being reached by what the school is doing." That group of teachers could set up a school within that school which ultimately, if the procedure works and it's accepted, would be a totally autonomous school within that district. This would be a school of choice; that is, no teacher would be forced to be in this subunit, and neither would any parent be compelled to send a child to this school. It would be a way for parents and teachers to cooperate with each other, to build a new structure. (Shanker, 1988)

Shanker's public and vocal support marks a turning point in the history of charter schools. Unlike an academic approaching the concept from a theoretical perspective (i.e., Budde), Shanker was known as a "tough liberal" and fierce advocate of teachers' rights and public education from an on-the-ground perspective. His endorsement added legitimacy to the concept of charter schools.

Special Education Statutes and Concepts

Special education policy grew out of the Civil Rights movement—specifically, the equal protections established under *Brown v. Board of Education* (1954)—and parent advocacy efforts, which led to the passage of key federal laws that continue to define the parameters of special education practice in U.S. public schools today. In 1973 Congress passed the Rehabilitation Act, Section 504 which prohibits recipients of federal funds (including public schools) from discriminating against individuals with disabilities (29 U.S.C. § 794[a]). The Americans With Disabilities Act of 1990 (ADA) built on this idea, and as part of its reauthorization in 2008 (as the ADA Amendments Act), Section 504 was subsumed within ADA (see Baditoi & Brott, 2014, pp. 9–14, for a detailed review of federal legislation relating to special education).

The Education of All Handicapped Children Act of 1975 (today's Individuals With Disabilities Education Act, IDEA) established a federal funding stream to help states provide services to children with disabilities. According to IDEA, public schools are the primary gateway to essential supports and interventions for young children and students with disabilities between the ages of 3 and 21. The No Child Left Behind Act of 2001 (which was a reauthorization of the Elementary and Secondary Education Act, now known as the Every Student Succeeds Act), and the 2004 reauthorization of IDEA, built on this framework by requiring schools to report on—and by holding them accountable for—the performance of children with disabilities on state assessments. Under current federal legislation and regulations, basic access and due process alone are no longer sufficient: Schools must also ensure that children with disabilities are making progress in achieving academic goals (34 CFR §300.347[a][1]; 34 C.F.R. §200.13[b]).

Key Special Education Structures and Constructs

Special education and related services such as speech or occupational therapy, are among services offered to students to meet their individual educational needs. Section 504 and IDEA establish key structures and constructs that shape how students with disabilities are educated, and outline a process to ensure that public schools comply with the law (see Table 1.1).

The myriad rules and regulations that guide how students with disabilities are identified and educated provide an overview of special education, but educating students with disabilities is more similar than dissimilar to educating all students. Effective instruction leads to student learning. However, successfully educating students with disabilities requires at least two things of practitioners. First, they must have high expectations and a deep understanding of how to teach and support students with a diverse array of needs. Second, administrators and policy makers must understand how to navigate the complex rules and regulations crafted to protect students' rights to public education.

State Special Education Statutes and Regulations

IDEA outlines state education agency (SEA) responsibilities to educate students with disabilities. In turn, SEAs are required to develop statutes and regulations to guide the implementation of IDEA. States are not permitted to waive federal laws, so IDEA requirements apply in all chartering states. In some states, special education statutes align very closely with IDEA, whereas other states have expanded upon the scope of the federal law to prescribe local practice in detail.

Special Education Enrollment Data

Students qualify as eligible to receive special education and related services based on their diagnoses with one or more of 11 disability categories identified in IDEA. The most prevalent disability is specific learning disabilities (SLD; e.g., dyslexia and dysgraphia), representing 40% of all students who receive special education services. According to the U.S. Department of Education (2014), in 2012 a total of 5.8 million students were eligible to receive special education.

Charter School Statutes and Concepts

A *charter* is essentially a contract between an authorizer and a nonprofit board seeking permission to operate a public school of choice. The contract outlines specific performance expectations and a timeline by which the school must meet them. The core tenet of the charter concept is that extending autonomy in exchange for accountability will

TABLE 1.1

Special Education: Key Structures and Constructs

STRUCTURE	EXPLANATION
Child Find	Under IDEA, school districts must identify, locate, and evaluate children with disabilities—a responsibility that resides with each state and which is typically relegated to local districts. Traditional school districts generally are assigned responsibility for a specific geographic area and are required to provide early intervention services to preschool-age children identified as having disabilities.
Individualized education program (IEP)	School districts (also known as local education agencies [LEAs]) must provide each child found to be eligible for special education with an *individualized education program* (IEP) developed by a team that includes general and special educators, specialists, and the student's parents. The IEP outlines the plan to meet the student's educational needs, including goals for student progress and the specific services the LEA will provide.
Free appropriate public education (FAPE)	Public schools are responsible for providing students with disabilities a *free appropriate public education* (FAPE). The constructs of "free" and "appropriate" education mean that children with disabilities are to be provided services and programs identified by their IEP team to meet their individual needs, and these are to be provided by the public education system, at no cost to the student's family. To date, Congress and the courts have defined FAPE as a continuum of services and supports necessary to provide a student with a disability access to the general education curriculum. The courts have not allowed LEAs to use cost to define what is "appropriate."
Least restrictive environment (LRE)	The principle of *least restrictive environment* (LRE) dictates that children with disabilities should, to the extent that it is possible and meets the student's educational needs, be educated in the general education classroom alongside their typically developing peers and provided with appropriate aids and supports, to maximize their access to the general education curriculum. LRE builds on the civil rights principle that *separate* is, by definition, not equal.

foster development of high quality and innovative programs in order to attract students who enroll by choice. Charter schools are created under state charter school laws which outline who is authorized to grant a charter and the extent to which charter schools are subject to state and local education codes.

> **The core tenet of the charter concept is that extending autonomy in exchange for accountability will foster development of high quality and innovative programs in order to attract students who enroll by choice.**

In 1991 Minnesota passed the first state charter school law. The Minnesota-based Citizens League's 1988 bipartisan report was influential to Minnesota passing the first charter school legislation in the United States. The law was enabling in nature; educators now had the opportunity to open a charter school, but no district was required to have one. The Center for School Change at the University of Minnesota's Humphrey Institute began assembling teachers and proposals for the first charter schools.

Recent presidents George W. Bush and Barack Obama supported charter schools as a necessary component of education reform and used charter schools as both a campaign talking point and legislative tool once elected to office (via the No Child Left Behind Act of 2001). Throughout the Obama Administration, Education Secretary Arne Duncan was a strong supporter, both in words and funding levels, of charter schools. As of 2016, all but seven states (Kentucky, Montana, Nebraska, North Dakota, South Dakota, Vermont, and West Virginia) had charter school laws in a variety of forms.

Over time, state charter school laws have grown more nuanced; the model law developed by the National Alliance for Public Charter Schools (NAPCS, 2009) has served as a blueprint for new laws (e.g., in Maine and Washington) and major amendments to existing laws (e.g., in Colorado and Louisiana). Although there are many similarities among state charter school laws (e.g., type of authorizers, requirements in charter applications, renewal cycles, and processes), state laws are highly idiosyncratic and reflect the outcomes of legislative processes that involve negotiations and compromises by various stakeholders, both for and against the creation of charter schools.

With few exceptions, questions and concerns about the extent to which existing policy parameters influence charter schools' ability to provide quality special education services has not generated much state-level legislation (Rhim & O'Neill, 2013). Since the launch of the movement, the key aspect of charter school law for the purposes of special education is the establishment of a charter school's legal identity as a school district, otherwise known as an LEA, or as part of an existing LEA (Heubert, 1997). Because IDEA assigns responsibility for educating students with disabilities to SEAs that, in turn, delegate most responsibility to LEAs, whether a charter school is its own LEA or part of an existing traditional LEA determines the manner in which the school serves students with disabilities.

Case Study: A New Day in NOLA

The Louisiana Special Education Cooperative
New Orleans, Louisiana

In 2008, Educational Support System (ESS) consultants Beth Giovannetti and Nancy Opalack received a U.S. Department of Education Charter School Program grant through the National Alliance for Public Charter Schools to determine the special education needs of the charter schools within the Recovery School District (RSD) and the students they served post-Hurricane Katrina. Giovannetti and Opalack first delved into the special education services being provided in the 23 charter schools in RSD and published a report, *The Special Education Project: A Study of 23 Charter Schools in the Recovery School District* (Giovannetti & Opalack, 2008), which outlined recommendations for next steps in increasing the RSD schools' capacity to serve a wide range of student needs. The Louisiana Special Education Cooperative (LA COOP), developed as part of the recommendations, now provides technical and service support, specifically focused on special education, for more than 40 charter schools in Louisiana.

"With the damage to other city-level systems after the storm, everything landed in the schools," Giovannetti said. "The needs in New Orleans post-Katrina were some of the greatest needs I have ever seen. A year after the storm, the mental health needs were unbelievably high and all of the supports had been washed away. Everyone had needs and everyone was trying to rebuild, all at the same time." According to Opalack, one of the biggest challenges and opportunities was authentically implementing a high-quality, fully developed continuum of services. "This community needed so much, and inclusion is not for everyone all the time." Being on the ground during such a transitional time provided an abundance of lessons learned:

- No one teaches you how to design and run a special education program, so it can be hard to build a program from the ground up.

- You have to actually go into the schools if you are going to help them build high-quality special education programming.

- If you don't know the culture of a school and a community, your recommendations will not match the needs of the school.

- It's important for schools to implement self-assessment and continuous quality improvement measures on a regular basis.

- It's important to build the special education capacity and confidence of the building-level teachers and administration.

According to a recent report (Hawf, 2015), from 2008 to 2013, the academic achievement of students with disabilities in New Orleans skyrocketed from an 18% proficiency rate to a 44% proficiency rate. Consequently, the 2013 graduation rate of students with disabilities in New Orleans rose to 48%, which is impressive when compared to Louisiana's overall graduation rate of 37%.

Legal status as an LEA or part of an LEA has notable programmatic and financial implications (Green & Mead, 2004; Heubert, 1997; Rhim, Ahearn, & Lange, 2007). Charter schools that operate as independent LEAs typically have greater freedom—and responsibility—in designing curricula, hiring teachers and staff, and implementing programs. Also, with a few exceptions, charter LEAs receive state and federal funds directly and have control over how they spend those funds to meet the needs of their students and programs. Charter schools that operate as independent LEAs are wholly responsible for providing students with disabilities a full array of services, potentially including a full continuum of alternative placements, analogous to a multi-school district. IDEA describes a *continuum of alternative placements* as

> Each public agency must ensure that a continuum of alternative placements is available to meet the needs of children with disabilities for special education and related services.
>
> The continuum…must—
>
> Include the alternative placements listed in the definition of special education under Sec. 300.38 (instruction in regular classes, special classes, special schools, home instruction, and instruction in hospitals and institutions); and
>
> Make provision for supplementary services (such as resource room or itinerant instruction) to be provided in conjunction with regular class placement. (34 C.F.R. §300.15)

Charter schools that operate as part of an LEA generally have access to a variety of services through the district (e.g., human resources, transportation, and legal counsel), on par with traditional public schools. As part of a larger, multi-school LEA, these types of charter schools are able to take advantage of the economies of scale realized when purchasing a variety of goods and services. Conversely, they may not be extended the same degree of autonomy as charter schools that operate as their own LEA; charter schools that operate as part of a district usually share responsibility for special education. In practice, this generally involves being required to adopt the district's approach to educating students with disabilities regardless of the extent to which it aligns with the charter school's mission. In some cases, this may include charter schools being required to adopt the established special education program provided by an LEA even if the district is operating under a court-imposed consent decree. For example, from 1985 until 2012, the Baltimore City Public Schools operated under a consent decree imposed by the U.S. District Court as a result of a class-action lawsuit filed by the Maryland Disability Law Center on behalf of students with disabilities in Baltimore City (*Vaughn G. et al. v. the Mayor and City Council of Baltimore*, 2004). The plaintiffs successfully documented that the school system had failed to conduct assessments of thousands of students and failed to develop adequate individualized education programs (IEPs) for the students (see Baltimore City Public Schools, 2012).

Embedding charter schools into a policy framework that assigns responsibility according to legal status—as an LEA or as part of an LEA—has been a challenge since the very beginning of the charter sector (Ahearn, 1999; Fiore & Cashman, 1998; Heubert, 1997). First, many state laws lack clarity regarding legal status. Some assign status according to who authorizes the school, leading to charter schools within the same state having different legal identities (Rhim & O'Neill, 2013). Although this diversity is not necessarily problematic, it introduces practical challenges when trying to integrate charter schools within the larger public education system. For example, some charter schools are invited to participate in district or intermediate district professional development opportunities and others are not.

Second, some states (e.g., New Hampshire and New York) define charter schools as independent LEAs *except for special education*, thereby further complicating the legal landscape and the definition of what it means to be an LEA. In general, existing structures (e.g., monitoring, reporting, and funding distribution systems) are ill prepared to manage the introduction of new single-school LEAs or autonomous schools within existing LEAs. In practice, this confusion has hindered policy makers' and practitioners' efforts to fully understand charter schools' responsibilities—as well as efforts to build charter school capacity related to enrolling and educating students with disabilities (Lange, Rhim, & Ahearn, 2008; Rhim, Ahearn, Lange, & McLaughlin, 2003; Rhim & Brinson, 2010).

The Current Landscape

The charter school movement is having a notable impact on the national education landscape. According to the NAPCS's 2015 report (2015b), the 2013–2014 school year saw the opening of 453 new charter schools and the closure of 210 failing charter schools nationally. This means that there are currently more than 6,400 regulated public charter schools across the United States, serving more than 2.5 million students (Rhim, Gumz, & Henderson, 2015). These numbers are stark when compared to the more than 89,000 public non-charter schools serving 46.6 million students in the United States. There is significant variability across the country both in terms of number of schools in individual states and the policy context in which they operate. That is, whereas some charter schools are extended significant operational autonomy (e.g., in Arizona and Ohio), in other states charter schools are extended relatively limited autonomy, operate as part of traditional districts, and, for all intents and purposes, are more similar than dissimilar to traditional public schools (e.g., in Maryland and Texas).

The number of charter schools in operation in 2013–2014 represented 7.3% growth in the charter sector (NAPCS, 2015). More than 50% of charter schools are in areas designated as cities or urban communities. Over 67% of existing charter schools are freestanding or independent charters, more than 20% are run by nonprofit organizations or charter management organizations, and 12% are run by for-profit organizations or education management organizations. Currently, over 89% of all charter schools are start-up organizations, whereas only 10% are conversion schools. Conversion schools are charter schools that started as traditional public schools or private schools and which have opted to turn into charter schools. More than 87% of all charter schools are nonunionized and only 4.5% are virtual schools. Almost 80% of all charter schools have been open for more than 5 years, with 35% of those having been open for more than 10 years.

Charter schools serve a variety of students: 35% of students attending a charter school self-identify as White or European American, 28% self-identify as Black or African American, and another 28% self-identify as Brown or Latino American. Almost 50% of students attending a charter school are eligible for free or reduced-price meals. Roughly 16% qualify as multilingual or limited-English proficient and 10.42% of all students in a charter school have an IEP (Rhim et al., 2015).

Students With Disabilities in Charter Schools

The extent to which charter schools are enrolling and serving students with disabilities has been an ongoing focus of criticism of the charter sector. A recent secondary analysis of the Civil Rights Data Collection (CRDC) confirmed that although there is a smaller proportion of students with IEPs attending charter schools than attending traditional public schools, the gap appears to be decreasing over time (Rhim et al., 2015). This type of data, however, does not provide insight into causation between type of school and the specific variables analyzed. There also is an element of subjectivity involved with eligibility diagnosis and service provision. For instance, from the CRDC data set it was not discernible whether differences between enrollment overall or by specific disability type result from different enrollment policies and practices or differences in the manner in which individual schools identify students as eligible to receive special education and related services.

> **A recent secondary analysis of the Civil Rights Data Collection (CRDC) confirmed that although there is a smaller proportion of students with IEPs attending charter schools than attending traditional public schools, the gap appears to be decreasing over time**

In the 2011–2012 academic year, students who qualified for special education made up 10.42% of total enrollment in charter schools, in comparison to total enrollment in traditional public schools, where 12.55% represented students who qualified for special education and related services; the national average is 12.47%. Students who qualified for services under Section 504 made up 1.53% of all students at traditional public schools and 1.52% of all students enrolled in charter schools (Rhim et al., 2015). According to the most recent U.S. Department of Education (2014) data, of students with IEPs enrolled in charter schools, 85% were placed in a general education setting compared to 67% in traditional public schools, and 13.45% of charter school students with IEPs have been suspended compared to 13.40% in traditional public schools. Charter schools reported expelling .55% of their students with disabilities compared to .46% in traditional public schools (Rhim et al., 2015). At the 2013 NAPCS Conference, Education Secretary Duncan stated, "I want to see charter schools [doing] a better job of educating students with disabilities" (Duncan, 2013).

State charter school laws have facilitated the creation of new schools devoted wholly or primarily to educating students with disabilities. Rhim and colleagues (2015) defined these schools as "charter schools with 25% or more enrollment by students with disabilities that self-identify as 'special education schools' and/or schools that report that 50% or more of their students qualify for special education" (p. 7). The National Center for Special Education in Charter Schools (NCSECS) verified the existence of 115 charter schools that focus primarily or entirely on students with disabilities. Just over half of these specialized charter schools have a general focus on disabilities (as opposed to a single disability type or a specific focus on two or more disabilities; Rhim et al., 2015). There are 49 schools that specialize in a single disability category (e.g., autism spectrum disorder, deaf-blindness). The greatest concentrations of these schools are in Florida (36 schools), Ohio (34 schools), and Texas (11 schools). Historically, these types of specialized schools have been called *segregated* or *alternative settings* and have been a topic of hot debate within the field of special education (Boundy, 2012).

The ideals driving policy and practice related to educating students with disabilities occupy common ground with the ideals of the charter sector: providing an education that fits students' individual needs and preferences. Nevertheless, the intersection of special education and the charter construct has been at times an uneasy union. Charter schools' autonomy provides a unique opportunity to innovate absent the ingrained systems and bureaucracies that can bind traditional public schools. Yet, 25 years of experience indicates that, in practice, many charter leaders have not fully leveraged this autonomy for the benefit of students with disabilities (Rhim & O'Neill, 2013). Multiple unique challenges influence delivery of special education and related services in the charter sector. Efforts to ensure that students with disabilities can access charter schools, and that these schools are positioned to offer strong academic programs for all students, are predicated on understanding and, to the extent possible, mitigating challenges unique to charter schools.

Equal Access

Ensuring that a student's disability does not limit access to education is a core tenet of federal disability law. The first step in the special education process is "Child Find," the IDEA mandate for school districts to identify, locate, and evaluate children with disabilities (20 USC § 1412[a][3]; see also Wright & Wright, 2007a; Wright & Wright, 2007b, pp. 206–207). States are responsible for developing a practical method to identify which students require special education and related services, and they typically delegate this responsibility to local districts. Charter schools that operate as LEAs are responsible for identifying students with disabilities who have enrolled in their schools. Moreover, traditional districts generally are assigned responsibility for a specific geographic area, which includes preschool-age students and students who do not necessarily attend the district schools, such as students who attend private schools, independent schools, parochial schools, or are homeschooled. The district is required to provide early intervention services to preschool-age students identified as having disabilities.

Enrollment Practices

As public schools, charter schools are required to operate open enrollment policies. Federal guidance related to the definition of a charter school explicitly identifies open enrollment or enrollment by lottery if a school is oversubscribed, as key defining characteristics of a public charter school (Heubert, 1997). Questions about the extent to which charter schools offer equal access to students with disabilities have been at the forefront of the charter school dialogue at the state and national levels since the early 1990s (see, e.g., Fiore, Warren, & Cashman, 1998; Garda, 2012; McKinney, 1996).

The issue of equitable access and quality services was the subject of a hearing by a Congressional committee (H.R. 4330, 2010) and the focus of a Government Accountability Office (GAO) report (2012). Using the most recent data available at the time (2008–2009 to 2009–2010), the GAO found that on average, traditional public schools in states with charter schools identify 11% of their population as having a disability, whereas charter schools identify 8%. The report identified potential explanations for the different enrollment trends (e.g., inadequate charter school funding, limited capacity due to size and newness, transportation issues, lack of parental knowledge of charter schools, preschool-age students with disabilities who receive services in the traditional district may not consider charter schools, and so on). The report also noted a distinct lack of information about factors underlying the differences and how they affect enrollment levels (GAO, 2012, p. 21).

Do enrollment trends in fact reflect discriminatory practices? To safeguard against this possibility, charter operators and support organizations must proactively develop solutions that address the source of the trends and spur development of exemplary programs. Examples of solutions being implemented include

- Examining special education policies and practices and implementing necessary revisions.
- Publicizing Child Find services offered by charter schools.
- Intentionally networking with local special education advocacy organizations.
- Developing thoughtful recruitment strategies that purposefully seek to encourage students with disabilities to apply.
- Explicitly including commitment to students with disabilities in recruitment materials.
- Investing in development of collaborative relationships with external entities to develop innovative service delivery models.
- Tracking and celebrating success of students with disabilities.

Although these strategies are presented as possible remedies, they are even more potent as preventive measures that should be part of exemplary authorizer and operator practice. Absent proactively addressing potential issues, charter schools are vulnerable to policies that foster bureaucracy but do not actually improve access or services to students with disabilities.

Proactive Practice or Reactive Policy?

Although the factors contributing to the differences require more in-depth examination to quantify impact, research and experience in the field indicates that multiple factors inside and outside the charter sector contribute to the differing enrollment trends (e.g., parental choice, IEP team recommendations, facility and resource limitations, lack of understanding of IDEA). Nevertheless, the charter sector would benefit from proactive introspection regarding the extent to which authorizers, operators, and support organizations are prioritizing equal access for all students.

Strategies that some schools have implemented to increase enrollment of students with disabilities include targeted recruitment efforts and focused outreach to special education advocacy groups and parent support networks. A number of states' charter school statutes permit schools to give students from specific groups (e.g., students enrolled in low-performing schools, students from high-poverty communities, students with disabilities) preference in enrollment lotteries. However, research to date has not documented states' leveraging these preferences to address enrollment concerns. Absent an intentional effort to recruit and retain students from a variety of traditionally marginalized groups, including tracking and documenting their outcomes, charter schools may increasingly be subject to policy making that hinders rather than helps their efforts to create quality schools for all students.

CHAPTER CAPSTONE

Opportunities for the Future

Highly functioning special education services, or lack thereof, can be a strong indication of the overall health of a charter school. Effective special education systems are reflective of a collaborative climate, accessibility, highly qualified staff, family satisfaction with the school, adherence to state and federal regulations, and functional data systems in place. Incorporating policies relating to the education of students with disabilities from the charter school's preauthorization stage (see Chapter 5), within an overall framework that protects both student rights and public interest and which ensures continuous monitoring of programming and services, can set the stage for effective education of all students in the charter school.

Historically, special education services across the United States have looked very similar because they have been provided within a context that has changed very little. Recent national reform efforts like the charter school movement and school choice initiatives have changed the educational landscape in ways unimaginable just 10 years ago. Many of the manifestations of reform efforts are offering the field of special education an opportunity to study the way services are provided, in a variety of new settings. Charter schools are on the important front lines of this effort, figuring out what special education "looks like" in a variety of new pedagogical environments and within different service delivery models.

Many of these changes have led to a variety of new hot topics for both special education and charter schools, including ensuring to make parallel charter schools comply with federal and state laws governing students with disabilities, addressing the use of exclusionary discipline of students with disabilities, offering a full spectrum of educational opportunities for all students, and ensuring all students have access to the best research-based new programs and pedagogies. These topics have plagued many educational settings and schools since the implementation of special education legislation. Both special education and charter schools must support research and development in authentic ways to ensure that students with disabilities are reaping the full benefits of educational innovation.

CHAPTER 2

Special Education Legislation and Funding

With Parker Baxter

The Individuals With Disabilities Education Act (IDEA), Section 504 of the Rehabilitation Act of 1973 (Section 504), and the Family and Educational Rights and Privacy Act (FERPA) are the main laws affecting the education of students with disabilities. These laws apply to all schools in the United States that accept any form of federal financial assistance—which charters schools do, through funding that either comes directly from the federal government or flows through the authorizer from the state department of education or the local school district.

As discussed in Chapter 1, some charter schools act as their own district, or LEA, whereas others are part of a consortium or the authorizer is the LEA. There are different implications for charters that are stand-alone LEAs than for those that are part of a district LEA. In a few states, charters are treated as their own LEA only for special education purposes. LEA status is, with few exceptions, explicitly defined in state law and has major ramifications for how charter schools operate and are funded with respect to students with special education needs.

IDEA

There is an extensive history in the United States of denial of educational services for students with disabilities. Prior to 1975, it was legal to prevent students with disabilities from attending public schools. This type of discrimination changed with the passage of Public Law 94-142, the Education for All Handicapped Children Act, later amended and currently known as the Individuals With Disabilities Education Act, or IDEA. There are seven main components of IDEA. Each one is very important to understanding special education, and all are of equal importance.

- Zero reject
- Nondiscriminatory evaluation
- Free appropriate public education
- Individualized education program
- Least restrictive environment
- Parental participation
- Dispute resolution and due process

All of these components work in tandem with one another, helping to ensure students with disabilities receive the services to which they are entitled and need in order to benefit from education.

Zero Reject and Nondiscriminatory Evaluation

The very name of Public Law 94-142, the Education for All Handicapped Children Act, was meant to emphasize that no child, no matter how severe the disability, was to be excluded from participation in—and had an expectation to receive a meaningful benefit from—education. In the years since the original law was passed, this idea has been expanded. Today, public schools have an affirmative obligation to look for students in their system who may have a disability and require special education and related services. As discussed in Chapter 1, under the concept of Child Find, schools have an affirmative obligation to test students who may have a disability for their eligibility for special education services. This evaluation may occur

- When the family enrolls the child in a school and indicates previous academic, social, or behavioral problems.
- When the child starts to engage in behaviors that impede her learning or that of others.
- When the child is struggling academically.
- When the child frequently misses school due to illness.
- When the child needs to go to a residential treatment facility for depression or substance abuse.
- When the family requests an evaluation.
- When the family provides the school with an evaluation from an outside or independent evaluator indicating learning or behavioral problems.
- When the child is not developing appropriate social relationships in the school.

This list is not comprehensive. However, each of these concerns may indicate, though do not guarantee, a need for special education services. Ignoring one of these indicators can cause severe educational harm to a student and may make the school susceptible to a compensatory education lawsuit.

IDEA's requirement for schools to conduct "a full and individual evaluation…before the initial provision of special education and related services to a child with a disability" (20 U.S.C. § 1414[a][1][A]) is intended to provide the basis for determining the student's strengths and needs. This process of evaluation includes prereferral, eligibility, programming, and accountability.

Prereferral. Not every student who is struggling in school or is perceived to have a problem needs special education services. Some students may just need extra tutoring, greater exposure to the content, or more one-on-one time with the teacher. It is important for all schools, however, to determine whether a student's difficulty rises to the level of potentially needing additional supports like those that can be provided by a special education teacher (Bateman & Cline, 2016b).

Students who consistently struggle with content or reading, are unable to sit still or attend to the task at hand, have difficulty following directions or remembering concepts or ideas from day-to-day, or have challenges interacting socially with other students, may in fact have a disability that is preventing them from accessing academic content. During the prereferral phase, teachers should work with struggling students, trying different interventions and keeping data about what works and what does not work (see Bateman & Cline, 2016a; McCarney, Wunderlich, & House, 2014). It is very important to try multiple strategies and approaches (e.g., a different classroom arrangement, visual schedules or task analyses, in-depth or repeated review of content), which often can help ameliorate the student's difficulty. Keeping data on strategies that have been implemented and the effect (or lack of it) on the student is essential in the event the teacher wants to refer the student for evaluation for eligibility for special education services.

It is important to point out that it is not just teachers who can request that a student be tested for special education—families can as well. Requests from a family to have a student evaluated for special education services must be taken very seriously. Charter schools must have processes in place for responding to such requests and for determining whether testing is warranted. If the school determines that the student is not exhibiting difficulty in the school setting, then it is reasonable to decide not to assess the student. However, schools need to pay close attention, particularly if the parents say the student is not enjoying school, having serious problems with an academic subject, or is being picked on or bullied by others. Again, these factors may not necessarily indicate that the student needs to be evaluated for special education services but they would certainly indicate there are problems that need to be addressed.

Eligibility and Programming. A student is eligible for special education services if there is a documented disability, the disability adversely affects educational performance, and the unique needs of the student cannot be addressed solely through the general education classroom. These three conditions indicate that the student requires specially designed instruction. A diagnosis from a physician or mental health professional provided by the family may be helpful but does not necessarily mean that the student is eligible for special education and related services. In order for a school to find a student eligible, there needs to be a comprehensive evaluation of information from the school setting (as well as the home) conducted by the educational professionals in the student's life. Only after a comprehensive evaluation is completed can the student be found eligible for special education (34 C.F.R. § 300.304). After a student is found eligible for special education, the information generated from the evaluation report is used to determine the types of educational supports the student will receive (see Chapter 3 and Chapter 5 for more in-depth discussion of individualized programming).

Accountability. All public schools, including charter schools, are expected to be able to demonstrate that they are providing effective instruction to their students. This not only ensures that schools are doing what they say they are doing, but it also helps the public at large to understand that progress is being made. Monitoring the progress of students who receive special education services is part of this assurance and also guides the school in refining the services it provides. Monitoring of LEAs, including charter schools, has changed since the 2004 reauthorization of IDEA and the No Child Left Behind Act of 2001 (a reauthorization of the Elementary and Secondary Education Act, now known as the Every Student Succeeds Act). Whereas the focus was formerly solely on compliance with processes, attention currently is paid to performance-based monitoring of students eligible for special education.

Free Appropriate Public Education (FAPE)

FAPE, one of the most important components of IDEA, stipulates that the educational services provided to students with disabilities are free (i.e., provided at public expense), that services provided must be appropriate for the individual student, and that the services must be provided by the local public school (20 U.S.C. § 1401(9)(A-C)). In the case of charter schools, this provision of support could be an arrangement between the school and other agencies or service providers. IDEA also requires that the services provided meet the standards of the state education agency (34 CFR § 300.17).

Individualized Education Program (IEP)

The IEP is the cornerstone of the services a student receives. It describes the specific special education and related services a student can expect to receive (see Chapter 5). The IEP team also serves an important role regarding placement, programming, and discipline decisions. A charter school that is its own LEA needs to follow all relevant state rules regarding IEP format, development, and timelines and is also responsible for tracking students' progress toward their IEP goals.

Least Restrictive Environment (LRE)

The basis of LRE is that, to the extent possible, students with disabilities are educated in the same setting as their typically developing peers. Public schools are required to provide supports in the general education setting to enable students with disabilities to access the curriculum; it is only when, even with such supplementary aids and services, the student is unable to satisfactorily participate that the school should consider educating the student in another setting (Bateman & Bateman, 2014). The goal for charter schools, therefore, should be to include students with disabilities to the maximum extent possible in the general education setting and work to have them become a part of all of the activities of the school when possible. If it becomes evident that the student is unable to progress in the general education setting, or that the student's inclusion in the general education setting creates an unacceptable degree of disruption for other students, the school should consider alternatives. It should be noted that this decision may not be based on the student's particular disability, the availability of required supports or services, space considerations, or administrative convenience.

All public schools need to ensure that they can provide a continuum of alternative placement (34 C.F.R. § 300.15), ranging from resource rooms, itinerant instruction, and small-group settings to in-home tutoring and instruction in hospitals and institutions. LRE does not mean that individual charter schools must be able to offer the full range of alternative settings in-house; this is not expected of regular neighborhood elementary schools, which frequently send students to other programs. The charter school, however, is still responsible for *providing* all the educational services, which may mean subcontracting with other providers. When making placement decisions, the charter school should consider the nonacademic programming provided and how moving the student to a different location or school might change the educational services the student receives. Figure 2.1 is a checklist to guide placement discussion and decision making.

Parental Participation

Federal law expects families to be heavily involved in the process of making decisions about the programming for and educational placement of students with disabilities. Specifically, "LEAs must establish and maintain procedures to assure children with disabilities and their parents are guaranteed procedural safeguards" (Bateman & Bateman, 2014, p. 18). IDEA delineates these procedural safeguards regarding notice requirements, consent requirements, the opportunity to examine records, and the right to receive an independent educational evaluation (see Table 2.1).

Dispute Resolution and Due Process

Parents of children eligible (or thought to be eligible) for special education services are entitled to multiple methods of resolving disputes if they are not happy with the school's programming or placement decision. These rights are afforded only to parents of students with disabilities, and do not pertain to children who are not identified as having a disability. Federal law provides for three types of resolution: mediation, resolution session, and due process hearing.

The purpose of **mediation** is to resolve complaints and differences about the programming and placement of a student who is eligible for special education and related services. Mediation is less adversarial than a due process hearing because the focus of mediation is coming to a signed, legally enforceable agreement that everyone can live with, instead of seeking a formal decision regarding what education is appropriate for the child. Mediation requires the participation of someone trained and impartial, who works to develop an agreement between the two parties using a collaborative problem-solving process. The mediator has no authority to impose a solution or plan on the school or the student (34 C.F.R. § 300.506[b][2]).

FIGURE 2.1

Placement Decision-Making Checklist

✓	CONSIDERATION	DESCRIPTION AND NOTES
☐	**General education supports**	What supports have been provided to the student in the general education setting?
		What supports have been provided to the general education teacher to support integration of the student in the classroom?
		Has the student benefited from these supports?
☐	**Additional support services**	If the student does not seem to be benefiting from current supports and strategies, what additional supports or services might be provided to assist the student?
☐	**Schedule**	If the student has been removed from the general education setting for part of the time because of intensity of services provided, is the student integrated with peers during the rest of the school day to the maximum extent possible?
☐	**Classroom management**	What is the effect on the student's peers of the services being provided to the student in the general education setting?
		Can services be provided with limited interruption and distraction?
☐	**Alternatives**	If the student is not benefiting from the general education setting, what alternative setting might be more appropriate and why?

TABLE 2.1

IDEA Procedural Requirements

Notice requirement	The parents of a student receiving special education services must be provided with a copy of the procedural safeguards notice describing the family's rights regarding their child's education and be kept informed regarding the student's progress.
	The procedural safeguards notice is to be provided to parents upon initial referral (seeking permission to evaluate), when the parent requests an evaluation for services, when the parent requests a due process hearing, or any time the parent requests a copy of information in the student's record.
	The procedural safeguards notice must include information about the procedure for filing for a due process hearing, timelines, participating in a resolution session, and information about mediation and how that can be pursued.
Consent requirement	Schools must obtain informed, written consent from parents before conducting an evaluation for special education services, before providing a student with special education services, and before conducting any re-evaluation of the student for special education services.
Opportunity to examine records	Parents must have the opportunity to review their child's records, including records relating to identification and evaluation of the student for special education services and educational placement.
	Schools are expected to preserve the confidentiality of information pertaining to students receiving special education services and to keep a record of all the individuals who access the files, including names, dates, and purposes.
Independent educational evaluation (IEE)	Parents have the opportunity to obtain an IEE from a trained examiner not employed by the school if they are not satisfied with the school's evaluation.
	Schools must provide parents with information on where to obtain an IEE and the criteria for IEEs. Parents have the right to an IEE conducted at the school's expense, if the school's original evaluation is deemed not appropriate.
	Schools must consider the results of an IEE when making decisions about special education services and placement.

When parents (or charter schools) request a due process hearing, a **resolution session** needs to be scheduled within 15 days in an attempt to resolve the issues or complaint prior to proceeding to a hearing. The purpose of this is to seek an agreement and collaboratively work to improve services for the child. The parties may agree, in writing, to waive the resolution session and go straight to mediation or a due process hearing. Resolution sessions include the parents and other members of the IEP team, along with a representative of the school who has the authority to commit funds.

If the parties reach agreement at the resolution session, the next step is to develop a written settlement agreement that is signed by both parties. There is a 3-day window in which either party may say they do not want the agreement, but after that it is enforceable in a court of law.

If the parties are unable to reach agreement through mediation or a resolution session, the next step is a **due process hearing.** The purpose of a due process hearing is to resolve disputes regarding the proposal to initiate or change a student's identification, evaluation, or placement. Hearing officers are appointed by the state education agency and are considered impartial; their role is similar to that of a judge. Both sides are usually represented by attorneys, and the process can be very time-consuming and expensive. In a due process hearing, evidence is presented, testimony provided, and the hearing officer's decision is binding (unless appealed) on both parties. Due process hearings exist as a check on the system to ensure students with disabilities receive an appropriate education.

Section 504

Section 504 of the Rehabilitation Act of 1973 is a civil rights mandate for all schools that receive any form of federal financial assistance and extends to individuals with disabilities the same kinds of protections Congress has extended to people discriminated against because of race or gender (29 U.S.C. § 794[a]). The intent of the law is to ensure that students with disabilities have equal opportunity and access to benefit from educational programs and facilities.

Because charter schools receive federal education funds, like other public schools they may not discriminate against individuals with disabilities, families, and the public at large. The responsibility not to discriminate applies to school administrators and all personnel who work (or volunteer) for the charter school. *Discrimination* refers to unequal treatment of qualified persons solely on the basis of their disability. According to Section 504, a person with a disability is someone who has "a physical or mental impairment that substantially limits one or more major life activities of such an individual; a record of such impairment: or being regarded as having such an impairment" (42 U.S.C. § 12102).

Although Section 504 is an anti-discrimination statute regarding students with disabilities, students eligible for accommodations under Section 504 are not generally the responsibility of special education staff and special education supervisors. School-level administrative leaders and general education staff usually bear primary responsibility for ensuring students who qualify for support or accommodations under Section 504 receive them. See Chapter 4 for more information on student 504 plans.

Section 504 and ADA

The Americans With Disabilities Act (ADA) was modeled after Section 504 and, in fact, uses the same definition of disability. The main difference between them is that whereas Section 504 applies only to entities receiving federal assistance, ADA covers most businesses and establishments—whether they are privately owned (e.g., private schools) or receive state and federal financial assistance. Thus, if a charter school is in compliance with Section 504, it is also in compliance with ADA.

Accessibility

Under Section 504, all new construction of buildings (since 1977) and construction updates must ensure physical accessibility. The intent of the law is that all programs and services offered by a school are provided in a manner that helps the integration of students with disabilities with their typically developing peers. Facilities constructed prior to 1977 do not have to be completely accessible, as long as the programs or activities of the school, viewed in their entirety, are readily accessible to individuals with disabilities. The full range of services offered by the school must be made available to the students, their families, and the public at large.

Note that "accessibility" includes parking and playgrounds. In 2010, the U.S. Department of Justice issued new regulations under the Americans With Disabilities Act Amendments Act (ADAAA; under which Section 504 is subsumed) containing specifics about parking regulations, including number of accessible spaces per total number of spaces. Specifically, accessible spaces must connect to the shortest possible accessible route to the accessible building entrance or facility they serve (U.S. Department of Justice, 2010).

Although ADAAA offers no specific definition of what makes a playground accessible, the American Society for Testing and Materials has published guidelines (2011) that provide direction on designing playgrounds and play equipment for accessibility and safety. The Department of Justice (2010) also offers extensive guidance on what is considered an accessible playground.

FERPA

The Family Educational Rights and Privacy Act (FERPA) is a federal law that protects the privacy of student education records; it applies to all educational institutions that receive federal funding. *Education records* are defined as records, files, documents, and other materials that contain information directly related to a student and that are maintained by a school or by a person acting for the school (20 U.S.C. §1232). They include such things as grades, class lists, students' course schedules, and disciplinary records. Education records do not include records made by a teacher for use as reference or memory aids (and not shared with others), personal observations, or peer-graded papers and exams prior to the grade being recorded in the teacher's grade book. Students are defined as both students who physically attend the school and those who attend remotely (e.g., via videoconference, Internet), but not prospective students or applicants. In primary and secondary educational institutions (i.e., K–12), all FERPA rights belong to the student's parent or legal guardian. However, when the student reaches the age of 18 (or begins to attend a postsecondary institution, regardless of age) all FERPA rights transfer to the student.

Under FERPA, students have four basic rights:

- The right to control disclosure of the student's education records.
- The right to review his or her education records.
- The right to request amendment of inaccurate or misleading portions of his or her education records.
- The right to file a complaint regarding noncompliance.

A student's education records may be disclosed only with the student's prior written (and signed) consent, which specifies the documents to be released, the purpose of the disclosure, and the parties to whom disclosure may be made. Charter schools that are part of a district LEA may share information with others in the district as long as it is necessary for education of the student.

Funding for Special Education

In 1975, when Congress passed IDEA's predecessor, the Education for All Handicapped Children Act, it was estimated that special education would cost approximately twice as much as general education; this estimate of the "excess cost" for educating students with disabilities provided the basis for the development of special education funding models. However, as IDEA is commonly considered the largest "unfunded" law ever passed (because funds were promised but levels have fluctuated, and have never reached the level stated in the law; see Bateman & Cline, 2016a), schools are often left wondering where the money is supposed to come from to

Increases in state special education expenditures over the years are primarily the result of an expansion of the student population identified as having a disability, rather than the cost of special education itself.

provide the special education services delineated in students' IEPs. Regardless, case law is very consistent that not having enough money is not a defense. As will be discussed in Chapter 4, the determination of what a child requires is an IEP team decision based on information developed from an evaluation report. It is not a decision that is to be based on what is available or what has historically been provided, and it cannot be based on the child's disability "label." It should be based solely on the needs presented by the child.

Federal special education funds are distributed through three state grant programs and several discretionary grant programs (see Bogdan, 2011). Part B of IDEA provides money to state and local education agencies to support them in meeting the special educational needs of school-age children (i.e., K–12) with disabilities. Part C provides money for infant and toddler programs and early intervention services. States, in turn, allocate funds for special education to LEAs in different ways (Bateman & Cline, 2016a; see also Ahearn, 2010)—based on pupil "weights," resources, reimbursement, flat grants, census, or actual expenditures (see Table 2.2). Federal funds are distributed in a manner that avoids encouraging special education over-identification; that is, to prevent schools from wrongly identifying low-performing students as "disabled" in order to secure more funds.

When Congress first passed its special education legislation in 1975, one intention was to ensure that 40% of a state's special education costs were covered by federal funds. If IDEA were "fully funded," states would receive the maximum grant, calculated at 40% of the national average per pupil expenditure times the number of children with disabilities served in that state in the preceding

> **It is very difficult to predict the true costs of providing an appropriate education, and most charter schools do not have the same range of resources as traditional public schools and school districts to meet students' needs.**

school year, adjusted for population changes. Under IDEA, the count of students with disabilities cannot exceed 12% of the state's total school population. It should be noted that increases in state special education expenditures over the years are primarily the result of an expansion of the student population identified as having a disability, rather than the cost of special education itself (see Bateman & Cline, 2016a). For fiscal year 2014, IDEA federal funding covered 16% of the estimated "excess cost" of educating children with disabilities. IDEA Part B "full funding" for fiscal year 2014 would have amounted to approximately $28.65 billion, or roughly $17.17 billion more than was actually appropriated. This shortfall in IDEA funding has been assumed by the states and local school districts.

TABLE 2.2

State Approaches to Distributing IDEA Funds

Pupil weight	Funding is allocated per student receiving special education services, either as multiples of the per-student general education amount or tiered dollar amounts, and may vary based on disability, type of placement, or student need.
	Some states allocate funds per student receiving special education services either as a single or multiple of the per-student general education amount or a fixed dollar amount.
Resource-based	Funding is based on allocation of specific education resources (e.g., teachers or classroom units). This is usually determined by prescribed staff–student ratios, which may vary by disability, type of placement, or student needs.
Percentage reimbursement	Funding is based on a percentage of allowable or actual expenditures.
Census-based	Funding is a fixed dollar amount based on the total enrollment or average daily "membership."
Flat grant	Funding is a fixed amount, per student or per unit.

Measuring Education Costs

There are two main methods to measure costs: input-oriented and output-oriented. *Input-oriented* measurement is based upon prescribing the resource inputs necessary for providing special education services. *Output-oriented* measurement methods uses existing data to understand costs and determine differences between current costs and future needs. Both are useful in helping to understand cost relationships when working with students with disabilities.

Ideally, all charter schools would have as much money as needed to provide services for students with disabilities to ensure that all students make progress toward grade-level academic standards. The reality is, however, that it is very difficult to predict the true costs of providing an appropriate education, and most charter schools do not have the same range of resources as traditional public schools and school districts to meet students' needs.

Managing Special Education Services

Given that the specific services provided to students with disabilities are dictated by the needs stated in the evaluation report and detailed in the IEP, cutting services is not often an option. However, charter schools can manage both services and costs by carefully planning their delivery of services within an overall collaborative framework. Working to address the needs of students with disabilities is a whole-school endeavor, involving all staff and support personnel, and incorporating additional outside resources as much as possible.

> **To be successful in responding to the needs of students with disabilities, the charter school leadership must clearly *define and express the belief that all students are valued* and need to be supported.**

To be successful in responding to the needs of students with disabilities, the charter school leadership must clearly **define and express the belief that all students are valued** and need to be supported. Providing schoolwide supports such as tutoring, positive behavior structures and interventions, and classrooms that incorporate universal design for learning principles meet the needs of students with disabilities but also provide a structure that enhances the education of all students.

Establishing a **respectful and cooperative working relationship** with and between special education and general education teachers supports all staff in meeting the school's expectations for their work. In a collaborative climate, all staff members feel empowered to seek support from others as well as offer their skills in team problem solving and providing support to students.

> **Establishing a *respectful and cooperative working relationship* with and between special education and general education teachers supports all staff in meeting the school's expectations for their work.**

Outreach, to both families of students in the school and the community, can further enhance a school's ability to expand resources and meet the needs of all its students. Developing collaborative, non-adversarial working relationships with parents, seeking out cost-sharing with other charter schools or agencies for specialty services, and carefully analyzing contracts with outside agencies can all lead to more efficient, focused special education services. Open communication with parents encourages their positive participation in the life of the school, enhances cooperative IEP development, and prevents misunderstandings that might lead to due process hearings.

CHAPTER CAPSTONE

Reaching Out

Outreach efforts should include families of general education and special education students, as well as the community. Providing appropriate services for students eligible for special education not only benefits students with disabilities but also helps all students. Funding provided to all schools should benefit all students. For more information about special education funding, see *Effective and Efficient Management of Resources* (Bateman & Cline, 2016a).

It is important to remember that IDEA is only funded at 40%, but implemented and regulated at 100%. This means that schools and families are constantly trying to figure out how to fill in the gaps. Funding gaps are not new; after signing the Education for All Handicapped Children Act in 1975, President Gerald R. Ford noted that "unfortunately, this bill promises more than the federal government can deliver, and its good intentions could be thwarted," because of what he characterized as "excessive and unrealistic" funding levels given concerns about balancing the federal budget (Freedman, Bisbicos, Jentz, & Orenstein, 2005). However, he promised that the federal government could create "a program that is effective and realistic," and committed to working "with the Congress to … design a program which will recognize the proper federal role in helping states and localities fulfill their responsibilities in educating handicapped children." Unfortunately, the funding gaps were never fully addressed and many of President Ford's concerns continue to plague the field of education when trying to ensure that all children have access to a free and appropriate public education.

CHAPTER 3

Supporting All Students: Instructional Programming and Administration

With Christy Wolfe and Kim Hymes

As discussed in Chapter 1, charter schools have a unique opportunity to provide innovative models of education reform and instructional strategies. The National Center for Special Education in Charter Schools (NCSECS) is one organization that brings together charter school organizations and special education advocacy groups to ensure that students with learning differences are provided equal access to these opportunities in the charter sector. NCSECS's goal is to advocate for students with diverse learning needs to ensure that if they are interested in attending charter schools, they are able to access and thrive in schools designed to enable all students to succeed.

One of the most important components of the education of students with disabilities is the concept of FAPE—a free appropriate public education. As discussed in Chapter 2, FAPE is one of the main components of IDEA; the intent is to ensure that public schools meet the educational needs of students with disabilities. Because charter schools receive public education funding, they are bound by law to ensure FAPE for their students with disabilities (see Table 3.1). This includes monitoring student progress, considering use of assistive technology, managing discipline issues, providing extended school year (ESY) support as needed (e.g., summer school), and incorporating the services of paraprofessionals and aides (34 C.F.R. §300.17). These aspects of FAPE, however, also provide some general guidance for charter schools interested in meeting the needs of all their students.

All students, not just those identified as having a disability, need to be monitored for their progress through the curriculum and provided with assistance if they are not meeting grade-level expectations. Progress monitoring can provide a clue as to the type of support needed for struggling students. It is essential when students are suspected of having a disability, as it will assist in determining eligibility for services, what sort of services to provide, and if these services are achieving the desired outcomes. All charter schools should strive to use information from student progress monitoring when making decisions about programming and placement, which not only benefits students but also helps teachers to plan instruction.

TABLE 3.1

FAPE Requirements for Charter Schools

TERM	EXPLANATION
Free	• A charter school may not charge the parents of students with disabilities for any of the special education services or related services delineated in students' IEPs. Free means "at public expense."
	• Charter schools may not refuse to provide the special education services outlined in an IEP because of the cost of the services.
State standards	• The state educational agency establishes acceptable standards for the provision of special education services to eligible students.
	• The special education and related services provided by the charter school must meet the state education agency standards.
Appropriate education	• "Appropriate" education is determined by the IEP team on an individual basis for each student receiving special education services. What is appropriate or provides educational benefit depends on the needs of the individual child.
	• The IEP is a contract between the LEA and the student's parents concerning the services that will be provided.
	• When a charter school develops an IEP for a student, it does not guarantee the student will meet the goals and objectives listed. However, the charter school is required to make a good-faith effort to help the student achieve those goals.
	• The signed IEP commits the LEA to providing the listed education services.

In an inclusive classroom setting, all teachers need to be able to respond to the needs of students with disabilities and other students considered to be at risk of failure. To be truly effective, charter schools should have dedicated special education staff and an administrator devoted to this purpose. In addition to appropriate professional development and supervision, teachers can be supported by paraprofessionals or instructional aides but may need training in supervising and managing support staff.

Many students with disabilities require a variety of specialized services which are typically provided by an interdisciplinary team of educators and related service professionals (e.g., general and special education teachers, paraprofessionals, speech-language pathologists, occupational therapists, physical therapists, school psychologists, school social workers, and school nurses). As noted in Chapter 1, charter schools do not need to be able to provide all support services required by the full range of students in-house; schools can make arrangements with outside vendors or agencies to provide specialized services.

Creating an Inclusive Environment

It benefits charter schools to proactively consider how they will address the needs of a wide range of learners, including students with disabilities, at various times throughout the chartering process and once the school is created. For example, at the initial authorization stage (see Chapter 5), schools should consider how they will ensure that federal and state laws related to students with disabilities will be implemented. Once established, consideration of the needs of students with disabilities should be reflected in hiring appropriate staff who can work with students with disabilities, and using teaching strategies that are accessible to students with diverse learning needs, such as those that follow the principles of Universal Design for Learning (for example, see the Center for Applied Special Technology website: www.cast.org).

All students benefit from a culture that is driven by inclusion that breaks through traditional stereotypes, and that sets high expectations. Historically, children with disabilities have been marginalized in their education, which has perpetuated myths that such students are unable to achieve and thrive in school. However, given the right services and supports, children with disabilities can succeed in school. Setting high expectations is critical to improving outcomes for students with disabilities. Charter schools have an opportunity to create positive learning environments for all their students, including students with disabilities. Intentionally reflecting on the school environment can help a school determine how it is serving—or can better serve—students with disabilities. The general questions in Figure 3.1 are intended to help start this reflective process and prompt future discussion among educators, administrators, and families.

> **Setting high expectations is critical to improving outcomes for students with disabilities.**

Recognizing and implementing research- and evidence-based practices also can help a charter school support all its students. Many instructional practices now widely accepted and implemented in general education settings (e.g., mnemonics, feedback, graphic organizers) were originally developed to support the needs of students with disabilities (Vaughn & Swanson, 2015). Similarly, a holistic approach which includes emphasizing a student's strengths, in addition to recognizing areas where a student struggles, addresses the whole child and perpetuates a climate that identifies students as "at-potential" rather than "at-risk."

> **Many instructional practices now widely accepted and implemented in general education settings (e.g., mnemonics, feedback, graphic organizers) were originally developed to support the needs of students with disabilities.**

FIGURE 3.1

Reflecting on the School Environment:
A Tool for Charter Schools

To ensure an inclusive environment for all students:		If yes, how does the school demonstrate this?
Does the mission, philosophy, and culture of the school promote inclusion of all students, including students with disabilities?	☐ Yes ☐ No ☐ Don't know	
Do the administrators and educators in the school understand the legal responsibilities associated with students with disabilities?	☐ Yes ☐ No ☐ Don't know	
Does the school provide adequate training to all educators on addressing the needs of students with disabilities?	☐ Yes ☐ No ☐ Don't know	
Does the school set high expectations for all students?	☐ Yes ☐ No ☐ Don't know	
Does the school communicate regularly with all families, and in a language they can understand?	☐ Yes ☐ No ☐ Don't know	
Are families and educators familiar with accommodations and assistive technology that can support student learning?	☐ Yes ☐ No ☐ Don't know	
Does every staff member see value in each student?	☐ Yes ☐ No ☐ Don't know	

Response to Intervention

Response to Intervention (RTI) is a multi-tiered approach to the early identification and support of students with learning and behavioral needs (Division for Learning Disabilities, 2008). The goal of RTI is to help all students by providing a base level of services and also intensive, individualized instruction as needed. RTI is designed to support making decisions in both the general education setting and when providing special education services, creating a well-integrated system of instruction and intervention guided by student outcome data. The main components of RTI are high-quality instruction, universal screening of all students, and providing struggling learners with differing levels of intensive intervention (see Table 3.2). Support for students is provided by general education classroom teachers, special education teachers, other specialists (e.g., reading specialists), and support personnel.

To fully understand RTI, one needs to understand the different tiers of support. There is no single model of RTI; a charter school can create its own model that incorporates the main components and is focused on improving student outcomes. In every RTI model, however, schools provide three tiers of support.

Tier 1: High-Quality Classroom Instruction, Screening, and Group Interventions

Within Tier 1, all students receive high-quality, scientifically based instruction provided by qualified personnel to ensure that their difficulties are not due to inadequate instruction. All students are regularly screened to establish an academic and behavioral

TABLE 3.2

Components of RTI

COMPONENT	EXPLANATION
Scientifically based classroom instruction	Charter schools should provide all students with classroom instruction based on research that uses systematic, empirical methods; relies on observational methods that provide valid data across settings and individuals; and which has been validated by rigorous, objective, and scientific review.
Continued student monitoring	Continually monitoring all students helps the charter school determine if certain students are functioning at or below their grade-level peers. It is important to use multiple data points to help determine the individual student's learning rate and level of achievement.
Multi-tiered instruction	For students needing more intensive services, charter schools need to be prepared to provide varying levels of intensity and support.

baseline and to identify struggling learners who need additional support. Students not showing adequate progress receive Tier 2 support and services (Division for Learning Disabilities, 2008).

Tier 2: Targeted Interventions

Students not making adequate progress in the general education curriculum in Tier 1 are provided more intensive instruction on the basis of levels of performance and rates of progress. Intensity varies across group size, frequency, and duration of intervention. These services and interventions are provided in small-group settings in addition to instruction in the general education setting. Students who continue to demonstrate difficulties at this level of intervention should be considered for more intensive interventions (i.e., Tier 3 support and services; Division for Learning Disabilities, 2008).

Tier 3: Intensive Interventions and Comprehensive Evaluation

In Tier 3, students receive individualized, intensive interventions targeting their specific areas of need. Students who do not achieve the desired level of progress in response to these targeted interventions should be referred for a comprehensive evaluation and considered for eligibility for special education services.

Progress Monitoring

Progress monitoring enables teachers to determine if students are benefitting appropriately from an instructional program. It can be used to identify students who are not making progress, and help plan programs for students who require any form of assistance (Bateman & Cline, 2016b).

Student progress should be monitored at least monthly and more frequently when trying to determine how students are responding to interventions. A teacher can graph the student's progress and compare it to expected progress and to the rates of others. Effective progress monitoring offers various benefits:

- Teachers are more aware of students' progress in the curriculum and meeting grade-level expectations.
- Teachers use data to make informed instructional decisions.
- Teachers can communicate more easily and accurately with families regarding students' progress, strengths, and challenges.
- Teachers and other charter school staff can use the information to determine whether to refer a student for referral for special education and related services.
- Teachers can provide enrichment for students who have already mastered grade-level curriculum.

To be effective, progress monitoring should be frequent but relatively short and easy to administer. Teachers should collect and graph data, and these data should be used to help make informed decisions.

If the school is effectively using progress monitoring, it has the data and information it needs to help determine whether the student needs periodic one-on-one services or special education and related services. Individualized instruction provides an opportunity for charter school teachers to work with students on a one-to-one basis to help students who have fallen behind as a result of academic problems, missed school, or content challenges. Continuous student monitoring enables a school to track the number of times a student requires individualized instruction, which could potentially be an important determining factor about whether the student needs more help via intensive instruction.

Accommodations and Modifications

As will be discussed in greater depth in Chapter 4, students with disabilities may receive classroom accommodations and curricular modifications via an IEP or Section 504 plan. An *accommodation* is a change in the course, standard, location, timing, scheduling, expectations, or student response that provides access for a student with a disability to participate in a course or test. An accommodation **does not** fundamentally alter or lower the standard or expectation of the content (Bateman & Cline, 2016b; see also Chapter 4). Accommodations can be thought of as physical or environmental changes, and can include

- Extended time on tests.
- Alternate settings (e.g., small group).
- Frequent breaks.
- Preferential seating.
- Reducing or minimizing distractions.
- Audio or large-print texts.
- Teacher-highlighted material and guided notes.
- "Chunking" instructions into steps or stages.

A *modification* is a change in the course, standard, timing, scheduling, expectations, or student response providing access for a student with a disability to participate in a course that **does** fundamentally alter or lower the standard or expectation of the course (Bateman & Cline, 2016a). Modifications can include

- Using a specialized curriculum which is geared toward the student's level of understanding.
- Simplifying texts by modifying the content area.
- Simplifying vocabulary.
- Basing grading on IEP goals.
- Altering assignments (e.g., lower grade-level or simplified text, worksheets, simplified vocabulary).
- Simplifying text on tests.

Providing Special Education Services

There are typically three ways in which state laws outline how special education is overseen in charter schools:

1. A charter school can be part of its local traditional school district, meaning that the traditional school district is ultimately responsible for special education.
2. A charter school can be its own school district, meaning that the school itself is responsible for meeting all special education requirements.
3. A charter school can partner with other charter schools in the area to provide special education, which results in joint responsibility.

Regardless of what special education structure governs its operations, every charter school should identify a primary staff member who is ultimately responsible for responding to questions, concerns, and compliance issues related to special education—from families, school staff, LEA administration, authorizers, and community members. This person would, in effect, be the spokesperson and leader of special education for the school. Having a single point of contact or reference can prevent situations in which different staff members give families (or other staff) contradictory information.

Special Education Administrators

Special education administrators are responsible for special education programming for an LEA and also for strategic planning related to the special education programming. *Strategic planning* covers a range of topics, including assessment, program development, enrollment forecasting, and compliance (Bogdan, 2011). A special education administrator provides support to principals and teachers at individual charter schools or to a group of schools under a charter. Support provided includes visits to schools regularly to discuss issues and to mentor teachers, as well as to offer guidance to help schools and classrooms implement services relating to students' IEPs or Section 504 plans. Finally, special education administrators also manage the business side of providing services, planning budgets, and monitoring costs. Individual school administrative teams are responsible for such tasks as managing in-house services, verifying that services billed by outside providers were actually delivered, and that the services provided meet the specifications of students' IEPs.

General and Special Education Teachers

Teachers have overall responsibility for the classroom and all the students within; they are the ones, on a day-to-day basis, who provide educational services for students. Special education teachers have primary responsibility for making sure the goals and objectives in students' IEPs are being addressed. Teachers often have to observe and monitor paraprofessionals, and work with students who are pulled out of the classroom for support. Teachers also require frequent professional development to help students get their necessary supports. Research has demonstrated that many charter schools include students with disabilities in the general education classroom for more of the school day than do traditional schools, making it important to understand how general educators and the special education team work together to support the needs of students with disabilities (Rhim et al., 2015).

··

Case Study: Racing Toward Responsive Teacher Evaluation

Goodwill Education Initiatives of Central Indiana
Indianapolis, Indiana

Goodwill Education Initiatives comprises 12 Excel Centers and Indianapolis Metropolitan High School. As the special education director for all of these sites, Tonya Taylor began exploring teacher evaluation methods that were authentic and responsive to the unique role a special education teacher plays. Based on her own experiences as a special education teacher in a traditional public school, she was familiar with common evaluation practices. "I had been a special education teacher evaluated under a general education framework, and I didn't want that for my special education teachers" she said. "I wanted to be able to give them non-punitive feedback about their performance in IEP meetings, co-teaching situations, and writing IEPs. There wasn't anything out there that we liked, so we created our own."

During her first year on the job she noticed conflicts between what she expected of special education teachers and what the site directors expected from them. Because of those obser-vations Taylor and Assistant Director Laura Cope developed a checklist site directors could use. However, they also realized that a more robust approach to special education teacher evalua-tion was an opportunity to innovate their practice.

Taylor and Cope's experience in developing new ways of evaluating special education teachers and enhancing their practice offers some guidelines for other charter schools and settings:

- Work with special educators to define the top things that a site director should see a teacher of record doing (e.g., case conferences, leadership, providing services). This not only serves as a springboard for the work but also gains buy-in from special educators, making them part of a team.

- As a basis for the special education teacher evaluation rubric, rewrite the general edu-cation teacher evaluation rubric, with each domain aligned to special education service delivery and implementation. The content of each domain should be specifically tailored to day-to-day responsibilities and skills of a special education teacher, as well as overar-ching goals.

- Involve both site directors and special education teachers in evaluating the draft evalu-ation rubric. Hold focus groups to gather stakeholder feedback, and incorporate when finalizing the evaluation process and forms.

- Hold a joint training for both special education teachers and site directors to ensure shared understanding of the process and its goals.

Taylor and Cope found that going through the process of developing a new evaluation system for special educators highlighted the need to "front-load" their support of special education staff by providing training, feedback, and support early in the process. Key to the success of this project were shared ownership of the work and ensuring that staff found a healthy balance between the "people part" of their jobs and their paperwork expectations. Since implementation, Goodwill has seen an increase in the effectiveness rates of their special education teachers and better services for their students. In the year after implementing the teaching evaluation rubric, their special education teacher retention went from 66% to 81%, and Goodwill doubled the number of graduates with IEPs. "Special education is no longer an afterthought," Taylor said. "We are a critical mass. The quality of the conversations between teachers and directors, and among sites, has increased dramatically."

Paraprofessionals

Paraprofessionals or instructional aides assist teachers in meeting the needs of students with disabilities. They report to the teacher and implement programs based on directives from the teacher. The help and assistance of another adult in the classroom can be one of the most important components of some students' programs, and many schools rely on paraprofessionals when providing special education services. The benefits to the school and to the student are great, with teachers being able to provide intensive supports for the student and paraprofessionals providing supplementary supports to both the teacher and to the student.

When evaluating support staff needs, the charter school should look at overall student population needs. What types of support do different students need, and what strategies are being implemented? How could a paraprofessional assist different students, in different settings?

> **The help and assistance of another adult in the classroom can be one of the most important components of some students' programs, and many schools rely on paraprofessionals when providing special education services.**

These considerations should lead to identifying the specific tasks the paraprofessional will perform, clearly defining job expectations, and providing a basis for training and performance assessment. The ideal paraprofessional is one who can work collaboratively and effectively communicate with others, adapt to different tasks and responsibilities, implement instructional and behavioral strategies, collect data on student progress, and adhere to overarching policies (e.g., confidentiality, security, and safety).

Implementing paraprofessional support can present certain challenges. Many paraprofessionals are not well paid, and the turnover rate in some schools is very high.

In addition, many paraprofessionals have not received a lot of (or even any) training or preparation for the role they will assume when working with students with disabilities in special education programs. Therefore, the charter school's general and special education teachers need to supervise and manage the work of paraprofessionals, including

- Planning, directing, and monitoring assignments and activities.
- Sharing insights and strategies.
- Supporting the paraprofessional as needed to clarify responsibilities, classroom routines, and scheduling.
- Communicating overarching school policies.
- Assessing performance.
- Meeting regularly to discuss performance and job expectations.

Cooperative Special Education Services and Vendors

Just like traditional public schools, a charter school or its LEA may need to contract with outside vendors to provide certain special education services. There are many reasons to consider an outside vendor or agency when providing services for students with disabilities. Some charter schools are small and lack the capacity to hire specialized teachers and staff to support students with low-incidence disabilities, whereas other students need only intermittent services (once a week or once a month), and still other students require services that are best provided by an existing, experienced agency. As noted in Chapter 1, individual charter schools do not have to be able to provide all services for all students in-house, but they do need to offer a continuum of services for students with disabilities.

Figure 3.2 is a checklist to guide decision making regarding contracting with outside providers for special education services. The first part of the checklist helps establish what types of support might be required based on the student population; the second part provides steps to guide contracting with outside agencies and other providers. There may be additional questions based upon the needs of an individual charter school; the checklist is intended to provide guidance in identifying primary considerations that should be addressed.

Charter schools need to be careful about how they spend their special education funds. Contracted services can be expensive. The school's obligation to provide appropriate services to students extends to the careful selection of contractors. There is a level of trust on the part of families that needs to be met. If families are unhappy with the services and support being provided by a contractor, their disagreement will be with the charter school, not the independent contractor. When contracting for services, the charter school is immediately responsible for ensuring that students with disabilities will receive an education that is appropriate to their individual needs.

FIGURE 3.2

Checklist for Outsourcing Special Education Services

PART 1: SPECIAL EDUCATION SUPPORT REQUIREMENTS

☐ Identify the specific, individual needs of all students eligible for for special education and related services.	Compare student needs for services to the capacity of the charter school to provide appropriate instruction and support. What areas of programming need to be addressed?
☐ Identify instructional or program needs that might be addressed in-house.	Consider different staffing patterns that might address unmet needs. Should you hire new staff? Are there current staff members who are capable of providing the services required and who might be reassigned?
☐ Identify instructional or program needs that might be addressed through the LEA.	If the charter school is part of a local education agency (LEA), what services are available from other partners within the LEA that might be tapped to respond to in-house programming needs?
☐ Identify needs unable to be met in-house or through the LEA, and identify outside vendors or agencies.	For the specific areas of instruction or programming that require support, research available providers within the community.
☐ Request preliminary estimates (e.g., costs, staffing, timelines) from potential vendors.	Compile information on costs and administrative work required in contracting with others. Develop a standard format for requests, to ensure comparison of similar activities. (For example, ask contractors to present a typical monthly bill of all the activities they are proposing, as opposed to comparing one's hourly bill with another's yearly bill.) Complete a cost analysis of all possible contractors, including indirect costs and administrative costs. Analyze the data to determine potential cost effectiveness; compare proposals of the different vendors to costs of possible internal services that the charter school can provide.
☐ Revisit in-house versus contracted solutions.	Continue to analyze services you are already providing through in-house staff or preexisting contracts. Which services are best provided in-house and which services are best provided by a contractor? When considering outsourcing activities currently provided in-house, what adverse effects (e.g., financial, morale) on staff would outsourcing create? What services should the school plan to provide in-house over the long term (e.g., high-incidence disabilities, community needs)?

FIGURE 3.2 *(continued)*

PART 2: CONTRACTING WITH PROVIDERS

☐ Develop a request for proposals (RFP).	The RFP should be based on in-house needs, not on the types of services contractors provide. The RFP should list the specifics of the services required, maintaining confidentiality of the students and families of the charter school. Have legal counsel review the RFP prior to sending to potential contractors.
☐ Evaluate proposals.	Review the responses to the RFP: Does the contractor's proposal directly address and respond to the needs of the charter school? Conduct extensive and detailed background checks of all proposed contractors. Follow up with contractor references and others who can speak to the contractor's performance and credentials. Does this contactor really have the capacity to provide the service required? Has the contractor provided this particular service before? What do others say about the contractor's performance? Consider administrative costs and in-house staff requirements to manage the outside contract. Does one contractor require a lot more paperwork than another? Is there a request for a deposit or payment prior to providing services? Are there extensive billing requirements? Have legal counsel review and provide feedback on highly ranked proposals.
☐ Develop a contract.	Ensure that contracts include multiple opportunities to check on the contractor's performance, that quality control measures are built into the system, and that the contract allows the charter school to cancel without undue financial hardship. Does the contract incorporate cost thresholds? That is, will the contractor be able to adapt to changes in services requested? If the contractor does not reach the cost threshold, do they keep the money overage? Have legal counsel review both a draft and finalized contract prior to entering into the agreement.

Note. There may be additional questions based upon the needs of an individual charter school; this checklist is intended to provide guidance in identifying primary considerations that should be addressed.

Extended School Year Programming

Although most ESY programs are held during the summer, ESY can be provided on weekends or through continuous virtual programming. The specific ESY services provided are based on the individual needs of the student. According to state and federal special education regulations, charter schools must consider ESY for all students with disabilities and make ESY eligibility determinations in a timely manner. The determination regarding whether a student requires ESY is based on whether ESY is essential to the student receiving FAPE—is the student making appropriate progress toward IEP goals? How much might the student regress as a result of an interruption in education programming. Does the student have the capacity to recoup skills or behavior patterns demonstrated prior to the interruption of education programming? These questions should be considered at every IEP meeting. If it seems unlikely the student will maintain skills and behaviors relevant to IEP goals and objectives after an interruption of services, the student should be considered eligible for ESY (Bateman & Bateman, 2014).

Like all decisions regarding special education services, ESY is based on individual student need, not on particular categories of disability or the school's convenience (34 C.F.R. §300.106[a][3]). In addition, schools must hold an IEP team meeting if the student's family requests consideration for ESY programming.

Communicating and Working With Families

Charter schools may offer distinct differences from traditional public schools and unique programming that appeal to families of students with disabilities. In the past, "back-to-school shopping" meant buying school supplies and uniforms, but in today's world, school shoppers are taking a more consumer-like approach to the school selection process. Since 2005, the school choice movement has presented families with new options regarding the education of their children. As the largest growth segment of the school choice movement, charter schools—now serving 2.5 million students in 6,440 schools, according to the National Alliance for Public Charter Schools (NAPCS, 2015b)—are becoming increasingly more commonplace, and thus are becoming an option for more families across the United States, including families of children with disabilities.

In 2004, the D.C. Opportunity Scholarship program gave School Choice scholarships to more than 1,700 public school students whose families were navigating poverty, as a way for them to pursue a nonpublic education for their children (Wolf, 2012). Since then, the program has grown considerably and now serves more than 8,400 students. A study by Michigan Future (Grimes, 2012) found that more than 71% of Detroit Public School families were using or shopping for school alternatives for their children, and the State of Indiana doubled the amount of vouchers available for the 2012–2013 school year over 2011–2012 (Beigh, 2012). Although the national landscape is changing quickly, there are roughly 18 voucher programs in 12 states, 14 tax-credit scholarship programs in 11 states, an educational savings account system in one state, and six individual tax credit/deduction programs in six states (Friedman Foundation, 2016).

In addition to voucher and choice programs, 42 states now have various forms of charter schools. As previously noted, because they receive public education funding, charter schools must be prepared to meet the educational needs of students with disabilities, and this should be clearly articulated and explained to families. Effective communication between families and charter schools is essential to supporting the needs of all students.

Case Study: Keys to Success for All Students

Christel House International
Bangalore, India; Mexico City, Mexico; Cape Town, South Africa;
Indianapolis, Indiana, USA

In many ways, charter schools have pushed a decentralized approach to education. Finding the right balance between adhering to a larger organizational mission and also being responsive to the individual community needs of different school sites can be a challenge. This model of service delivery is a distinguishing feature of the Christel House International organization. As Caitlin Teague, director of Programs and Services, said, "We are really trying to find the right balance between standardization and local control." This task becomes more daunting given that Christel House International serves students across four countries. All four sites share the primary mission of serving students born into poverty, and all provide robust special education services as a means to meet this mission.

Special education across four countries is an ambitious and admirable goal. A component of achieving this goal has been the financial support from a private donor. One donor, in honor of her daughter with learning disabilities, provides assistance solely for ensuring services to support the lowest achieving 35% of all Christel House students. This support has enabled Christel House to develop, implement, and continually evaluate the effectiveness of the services provided for students with identified learning differences, as well as offer programs that blur the lines between special education and general education.

All school sites start with an intake process that adheres to the local government policies and regulations. At the time of entrance, all students are tested to determine their learning strengths and needs, and to set a diagnostic baseline. Tests are chosen by each site and are based on fidelity, validity, reliability, and regulatory processes within the local context. Schools use the data to make appropriate class placement decisions and as an initial data point for tracking each student's holistic growth. Each site employs professional development for teachers, RTI-like services to support students prior to a formal diagnosis, psychological testing as necessary, a site-specific IEP document, and college or career support after graduation. Christel House students participate in their local and national standardized tests.

These elements appear to be effective across all sites; the key to this success appears to be the flexibility each site has within this framework.

- Christel House India promotes its special education services as a recruitment tool. Currently, the government of India does not offer any subsidies for special education services, and public schools do not offer these types of supports. Government policy also forbids screening or testing of any kind prior to admissions. Approximately 10% to 12% of students in India qualify for special education services. One special education teacher and two interventionists are employed to provide "push in" services. Christel House India boasts a 92% college and job placement rate for graduates, a 100% pass rate on the 10th-grade board exam, 94% pass rate on graduation exams, 96% daily attendance rate, and 98% retention rate.

- Christel House Indianapolis comprises four sites, all of which are charter schools authorized by the Indianapolis Mayor's Office. Like other Christel House sites, the U.S. charter schools focus on early intervention and motivation. They provide proactive and pre-emptive services to students starting with a kindergarten "jump start" program that starts before the regular school year, early diagnostic supports, focused and data-driven RTI services, mastery requirements for advancement, and ESY services in the summer. Supports are deliberately fluid, so students can access any of the supports they need to be successful. The schools also have a robust special education department that provides services to students once a disability has been identified. Currently, Christel House Indianapolis has a 92% pass rate on the state-mandated third-grade reading test, a 95% average daily attendance rate, an 80% retention rate, an 83% pass rate in math, and an 80% pass rate in language arts.

- Christel House South Africa exists in the midst of a nationwide movement to eliminate specialized schools and toward a new inclusionary model incorporated in South Africa's laws. In South Africa, a student's right to move from school to school is protected by the national constitution. Approximately 40% of students at the school identified after admission as having learning difficulties. The school employs three special education teachers; in addition, the Ubuntu philosophy of "Your child is my child is everyone's child" provides a framework for collaboration, recognizing the give and take between individualism and community. The school hosts class community meetings, attended by families and students, during which the discussion focuses on how each member of the class community can help support the class. Christel House South Africa boasts a 73% pass rate on the national systemic test in a country where the average pass rate is 15%, a 98% retention rate, a 98% daily attendance rate, and a 98% graduation rate.

- Christel House Mexico provides classes in English, but most activities and communications are in Spanish. Currently, 25% of the school's students qualify for special education services, which are provided by a special education coordinator, a pedagogist, and a special education teacher. In Mexico, student test scores are used to calculate school evaluations, not students; schools are forbidden from talking to students about their individual test scores. Schools are, however, required to give students grades and report cards as individual evaluation methods. Christel House Mexico has a 96% student retention rate, a 98% daily attendance rate, a 100% pass rate on the high school entrance exam, a 2% insufficient rate in lower-grade language arts, a 1.7% insufficient rate in lower-grade math, a 7% upper-grade insufficient rate in language arts, and a 5% upper-grade insufficient rate in math—making it the highest-ranked school in its geographic district.

By providing schools a scientifically sound and culturally responsive framework within which to work, Christel House International has created a decentralized approach to special education that works across borders and learning needs.

Charter School Policies and Procedures

The charter school's mission, philosophy, focus, or educational approach should be clearly delineated in all promotional and informational material (e.g., its brochures and website). This helps families determine whether the school is a good "fit" for the student and his or her individual needs. Information such as the criteria for admission and admission process, average class size, teacher qualifications and staffing, curriculum levels (e.g., honors, AP), extracurricular activities, use of technology in the classroom, student population demographics, disciplinary procedures, and nontraditional learning environments (e.g., virtual or blended learning) also helps families make educational decisions for their children.

Because they receive public education funding, charter schools must be inclusive of students with disabilities and, because students with disabilities often require specialized instruction, it is important for families to understand the school's perspective on addressing such needs. Charter school staff and families should share an understanding about how special education and students with disabilities are viewed in the school community. Ultimately, when a charter school is a good fit for a family and student, the family and educators will hold common beliefs on school expectations for and obligations to students with disabilities. Charter schools should be prepared to provide families with information on their policies and practices regarding students with disabilities, including

- The school's approach to ensuring an inclusive environment for all students, including instructional strategies designed to accommodate the needs of different learners, school climate and culture, and the use of assistive technology.
- The qualifications, availability, and experience of general and special education staff members.
- How student progress is monitored, and how the school communicates with families regarding student progress in the curriculum.
- Accessibility features that allow for physical access in the school building, classroom, administrative space, and external spaces.

- Accessibility in learning, including making educational materials available in an accessible format.
- The process for identifying and evaluating students to determine whether they are eligible to receive special education and related services.
- Processes to develop and implement an IEP for students who qualify for special education services, or a Section 504 plan for students who need accommodations (see Chapter 4). How the school responds to the needs of a student with an IEP or 504 plan who transfers from another school.
- The school's dispute resolution process for resolving disagreements regarding student educational plans.

In addition, schools should be prepared to respond to inquiries relating to the performance of students with disabilities on statewide assessments, the rate of disciplinary referrals (e.g., suspensions, expulsions), students' graduation rates, and their postsecondary outcomes. For charter schools that are solely elementary school and do not offer a high school curriculum, families may want to know how the transition to another level of schooling is managed.

Responding to Inquiries From Families

When approached by a family member of a student with a disability, the charter school should respond by seeking additional information on the student and her individual needs. This should be in the spirit of exploration and getting to know a potential student, rather than an attempt to dissuade a family because the student's needs seem greater than the school's current capacity to meet. Asking the family a series of questions about their own preferences and the student's strengths and needs helps maintain open communication and provide initial information that can assist the charter school in planning to meet the needs of this individual student—and potentially other students with similar challenges. For example

- What is the student's disability?
- What special needs or requirements does the disability present?
- What strategies have worked with the child before? What related services has the child received?
- What areas of academics is the child interested in?
- Does the student have a particular interest in the arts? STEM (science, technology, engineering and mathematics)? Sports? Foreign languages?
- Does the student currently have or need a flexible schedule due to his disability?
- Does the student require nursing care?

Maintaining open lines of communication with the family of a student with a disability is important to ensuring that all of the student's needs are being met.

Case Study: Taking Care of Business

New York City Special Education Collaborative
New York, New York

Founded in 2004, the New York City Charter School Center is a leader in the New York City charter school movement. One of the many programs offered by the Charter School Center is the NYC Special Education Collaborative, a membership organization that empowers schools to develop high quality, inclusive special education programs by providing training, professional development, resources, support, and guidance. The Collaborative serves more than 180 charter schools citywide, with approximately 15% of students having a diagnosed disability.

Dixon Deutsch, vice president at the NYC Charter School Center, believes that charter schools provide special educators an environment where they can move, from being focused mainly on compliance, toward innovation and best practices. "We operate like a start-up," he said. "We do market research, we pilot a lot of things to see what the sector will respond to, we give ourselves 'head space' to be creative and figure out new solutions to old problems."

As a large membership organization, the Collaborative has also embraced its role as an advocate within the city for high-quality special education services. "We want to make an impact, so we have solidified our relationship with the New York City Department of Education, and we advocate for our schools in the policy arena. Most recently we worked with the mayor's office to ensure that our city's special education policy is aligned with federal guidelines, through a budget increase for meeting compliance mandates," Deutsch added.

Deutsch's top tips for running an effective special education collaborative include

- Mind-set is everything! Charter school leaders should not only believe but also understand why high quality special education is good for everyone in their building.

- Classrooms are where you close the achievement gap, not professional development. Supporting high-quality instruction in engaging classrooms is key.

- You must know your schools, your community, and your resources very well.

- To sustain high quality services requires roots in both special education and business. You need to know about price structures, scalability, and your marketplace. You need to have an entrepreneurial spirit, in addition to knowing the building-level application of special education services.

- Your offerings should evolve as your schools grow in their practice.

Best Practices in Working With Families

Using plain language and making information easy to access is essential to having a meaningful dialogue with families. Just as in traditional public schools, a family's positive relationship with educators in a charter school is important for a child's success. The strategies presented in Table 3.3 can help foster collaboration between families and charter schools.

As discussed in Chapter 1, charter schools must adhere to federal and state laws governing how special education services are provided to students with disabilities. One of the core aspects of federal legislation and regulations is the concept of consent; the family must be fully informed of all information regarding potential identification and evaluation of the student, and agree in writing to any activities for which consent is being sought (34 C.F.R. §300.9). Parents also have the right to disagree with the decisions of the school and can seek outside reviews to determine if the school is, in fact, providing an appropriate education to a student with a disability. The school must inform them of this right.

> **It is the school's responsibility not only to ensure that families are granted these rights but also to ensure that families understand their rights.**

In addition, families have a variety of other rights, including the right to request testing, to contribute information that might be relevant when considering eligibility, to request an independent educational evaluation and ask that its results be considered when making determinations regarding programming and placement, and to bring others to meetings regarding a student's educational programming. It is the school's responsibility not only to ensure that families are granted these rights but also to ensure that families understand their rights.

TABLE 3.3

Working With Families

BEST PRACTICE	RATIONALE
Start early	As soon as a student with a disability is accepted into a charter school, initiate a conversation between the family and educators to begin planning for the upcoming school year. Starting this conversation early can help both families and educators start the year off positively. To help all involved better understand the needs of the student, it is helpful to have copies of any recent neuropsychological testing, previous IEPs, or other documents. This conversation is an excellent opportunity to have the new team discuss every party's goals, dreams, and aspirations for the school year and beyond.
Work together	Families and schools should work together to think about a student's strengths and challenges, including identifying strategies that have worked well—or not so well—in the past when planning for the future. Getting to know a new student is a priority for the charter school, and any information families can provide about the child's learning style, behavior, or social attributes can be helpful in starting the year off positively. Throughout the year, families and educators should continue to communicate observations about strategies that resonate with the student.
Involve students	Helping students understand the importance of recognizing what they need and asking for it—a skill known as self-advocacy—may take time and practice to master but allows students to take ownership of their learning, communicate their needs to help accomplish their goals, and build their self-confidence. Together, schools and families can encourage children to consider solutions to their challenges and help them understand appropriate ways of communicating their needs.
Monitor progress	It is important for families to understand how progress will be measured against the student's IEP or Section 504 plan and the process for updating the individual student's education plan. These documents serve as the blueprint for the individualized instruction and accommodations provided to the child. The family and school team should have a mutual understanding of the frequency with which student plans are implemented and updated.

CHAPTER CAPSTONE

Home–School Partnerships

Educating students with disabilities is both a legal requirement and a moral imperative for every school, including
charter schools. As the charter school movement continues to
grow throughout the United States, families will have new decisions to make regarding
which public school their children attend. For all families—especially those with children
who have special education needs—this new decision-making process can benefit from a
better understanding of the specific charter school and its unique traits and opportunities.
To be a truly viable choice for all families, charter schools have a responsibility to create inclusive learning environments guided by having high expectations for all students,
including those with disabilities. Forging a productive home–school partnership will help
ensure that all students, including those with disabilities, have the opportunity to thrive in
the classroom and beyond.

Education researchers have spent a considerable amount of energy examining the
relationship between schools and families. Much of their research has focused on
understanding what schools can do to partner with families to support students' academic
achievement. In this new era of choice and competition, understanding and building
relationships with families is only part of the story. Charter schools need to know why
families choose a particular school, why they stay, and why they leave. Strong relationships with families are critical to student retention.

CHAPTER 4

Individualizing Education: IEPs and Section 504 Plans

With Scott Bess and Christy Wolfe

As discussed in previous chapters, a student with a disability who is eligible to receive special education and related services does so via an individualized education program (IEP). A student with a disability who is not eligible for special education services but nonetheless requires accommodations in order to access the curriculum is supported via a Section 504 plan. Both IEPs and 504 plans are binding; charter schools are required to develop and implement plans appropriate to an individual student's needs. It is important to understand that IEP and Section 504 plans are more than paperwork compliance documents; they guide the programming and accommodations provided for students with disabilities.

IEPs

As Creighton Martin and Hauth have noted (2015), "The cornerstone of special education is instruction that is specifically designed to meet the unique needs of students with disabilities" (p. 84). The IEP is a written document that sets forth the special education services that eligible students are to be offered as a part of their individualized programming and related services under IDEA. The IEP provides a comprehensive statement of the educational needs of a child with a disability and the specially designed instruction and related services to be employed to meet those needs (*Burlington School Committee v. Massachusetts Department of Education*, 1985). The IEP is developed in response to needs demonstrated by the student (e.g., via behavior, academic struggles, language issues) and describes how those needs will be met (e.g., behavior plan, academic intervention, communication or assistive technology support). The student's educational plan, as described by the IEP, is developed through the collaborative effort of the parents, the student with a disability, school personnel, and service providers—together, *the IEP team.*

There is no single "master" form for an IEP. Within states, and even within school districts within a state, schools use different forms and methods of compiling the components of a student's plan. However, there are nine required elements all IEPs must include (Bateman & Herr, 2006; see Table 4.1).

TABLE 4.1

Nine Required Elements of an IEP

ELEMENT	EXPLANATION
Present level of performance	A statement of the student's present levels of academic achievement and functional performance (known as PLAAFP), including how the disability affects the student's involvement and progress in the general education curriculum.
Annual goals	A delineation of measurable annual academic and functional goals, designed to meet the student's needs and respond to the challenges presented by the student's disability. Goals must be designed to support the student's progress in the general education curriculum.
Progress monitoring	A description of how the student's progress toward meeting the annual goals will be measured; covers timing of periodic progress reports (e.g., at same time as academic report cards for other students).
Services to be provided	A statement of the special education and related services and supplementary services to be provided. Services should support the student in advancing appropriately toward attaining the annual goals, being involved in and making progress in the general education curriculum, and participating with typically developing peers. Includes related services, if any are needed.
Program modifications or supports	A description of curricular modifications and supports that can be utilized by school personnel in providing the services to the student to enable that student to meet annual goals and to participate in school activities.
Nonparticipation in school activities	An explanation of the extent, if any, to which the student will not participate with his typically developing peers in the general education setting, and in extracurricular and nonacademic activities. Is there a plan for future integration into these activities?
Assessment accommodations	A statement of any individual accommodations required to measure the academic achievement and functional performance of the child on district and state assessments.
Alternate assessment	If the IEP team determines that the child should take an alternate assessment instead of the standard state or district assessment, the IEP must include a statement of why the child cannot participate in the regular assessment and why the particular alternate assessment selected is appropriate for the child.
Dates of service	The projected date for the beginning of the services and modifications, and the anticipated frequency, location, and duration of those services and modifications.

There are IDEA regulations that are specific to charter schools (Notice of Final Priorities, Requirements, Definitions, and Selection Criteria; Charter Schools Program Grants to State Educational Agencies, 80 FR, 34201). These regulations stress that students with disabilities retain all rights described in other sections of the law.

How a charter school is classified under applicable state law determines the implementation of special education rules and regulations for the school. If the charter school is considered part of a larger charter school organization, that larger district has obligations for ensuring that the charter school adheres to the law. If the charter school is considered a local education agency (LEA), the charter school has responsibility for developing and implementing student IEPs. If the school is part of an LEA, the LEA must

> serve children with disabilities attending those charter schools in the same manner as the LEA serves children with disabilities in its other schools, including providing supplementary and related services on site at the charter school to the same extent to which the LEA has a policy or practice of providing such services on the site to its other public schools. (34 C.F.R. § 300.209)

—as well as provide funds on the same basis as they are allocated to the LEA's other public schools. If a charter school is an LEA (or not an LEA or part of an LEA, but otherwise also receives funding directly), it is responsible for ensuring that it fulfills the requirements of the law pertaining to educating students with disabilities.

FAPE and Progress Monitoring

As noted in previous chapters, the concept of FAPE is a cornerstone of IDEA. Because schools must ensure that students with disabilities receive FAPE, school administrators should regularly reflect on whether they are providing appropriate services to their students with disabilities. If it appears a student is not receiving FAPE, the IEP team must immediately convene and identify changes to ensure the student receives the necessary services that will help promote progress on the IEP goals and objectives.

Much of the determination about whether a student is receiving FAPE is a *process* definition, meaning a determination of whether the appropriate policies and procedures are being followed in a timely fashion by individuals certified for the job they are performing (Bateman & Bateman, 2014). It is very important to make sure timelines are followed and the correct people are providing the necessary services. It is also important for the student to be making progress through the curriculum. If the student is not making progress, the IEP may need to be changed and the level and or type of service may need to be adjusted to help the student. Figure 4.1 is a checklist to support charter school administrators in determining whether a student is receiving FAPE (see Bateman & Bateman, 2014).

FIGURE 4.1

Questions to Determine and Establish FAPE

QUESTION			EVIDENCE/EXPLANATION
Was the student evaluated in a nondiscriminatory fashion?	☐ Yes	☐ No	
Are all those providing services certified for their roles in developing and implementing the IEP?	☐ Yes	☐ No	
Has the student's family (and the student, if age 16 or older) been involved in every stage of the development of the IEP?	☐ Yes	☐ No	
Has the student's parent or guardian been informed of due process rights?	☐ Yes	☐ No	
Is the IEP individualized?	☐ Yes	☐ No	
Does the IEP list necessary related services?	☐ Yes	☐ No	
Are all IEP components being implemented?	☐ Yes	☐ No	
Is there clear documentation of the level of functioning of the student in comparison to the goals and objectives on the IEP?	☐ Yes	☐ No	
Are all the objectives of the IEP written with both academics and behavior in mind?	☐ Yes	☐ No	
Is the student receiving educational benefit from the program?	☐ Yes	☐ No	
Does the student participate in the academic and extracurricular activities of the school with typically developing peers, to the maximum extent possible?	☐ Yes	☐ No	
If the student does not participate with typically developing peers, is there a plan for his or her future integration into school activities?	☐ Yes	☐ No	

Purposes Served by the IEP

The IEP is a document that delineates the services required by a student with a disability and how these services will be provided. A student's IEP is developed by a team that must include a representative of the school (e.g., principal), general and special education teachers, a person knowledgeable about the student's evaluation, related services personnel as needed, the parent or guardian, and the student (beginning at least at age 16, if not before). The IEP serves a variety of interrelated purposes.

Communication. The IEP provides information to administrators, teachers, and the student's family about the special education services the student will receive. As discussed in Chapter 2, parental involvement and participation is one of the central tenets of IDEA and is directly defined and outlined in the law (34 C.F.R. § 300.322). The IEP ensures that everyone associated with supporting the student understands how that is to be done.

Administration. Clearly written IEPs assist schools in effectively implementing the educational plans they outline. By reviewing student IEPs as a whole, the charter school can identify trends among student needs that affect staffing decisions. As discussed in Chapter 3, students with disabilities are supported by teachers (general and special education), specialists, and paraprofessionals. The IEP will also list related services a student is expected to receive, which may include transportation, speech therapy, or physical therapy. Charter school administrators need to review IEPs for such related service requirements to administratively plan for coverage or for outsourcing such services (see Chapter 3).

As part of its administrative responsibilities, the charter school must ensure that IEPs are developed in an appropriate timeframe with all appropriate people contributing, and that student IEPs are reviewed and revised at least annually. If the student is not making progress, the IEP should be revised more frequently, depending upon the needs of the student. The burden of responsibility is solely the school's to ensure that a student's IEP is written in a timely fashion, is appropriate, and is implemented.

Compliance. It is the charter school's responsibility to make sure the services written in the IEP are being delivered to the student. Although a student's family members are a part of the team developing the IEP, they are not responsible for implementation of services. In addition, the school cannot expect or require a student's family to provide any of the services required by the student; this, too, is solely the school's responsibility.

Monitoring. Charter school administrators must periodically check to make sure the IEP is being implemented and the related services are being delivered. It is much better for a charter school to determine an IEP is not being implemented than to have parents or an outside compliance monitor make that determination. Chapter 3 provides additional information on the purposes and uses of effective progress monitoring.

Schools are required to monitor and evaluate whether students are making progress toward IEP goals and objectives, as part of establishing whether the program as written is supporting the student's progress. Effective monitoring also reveals if programming for a student needs to be adjusted. Did the student master the goals and objectives

> **It is much better for a charter school to determine an IEP is not being implemented than to have parents or an outside compliance monitor make that determination.**

sooner than was expected? Does the student still need the specified special education and related services? Progress toward the IEP goals and objectives is an important determination of whether the student's program needs to be changed. Maybe the student needs more intensive services, or maybe the student was misdiagnosed at a previous school (e.g., as a student with a learning disability when she actually should have been diagnosed as having autism spectrum disorder). Data on progress toward IEP goals— in addition to notes and comments from teachers and others working with the child— is essential for establishing a need for continued special education services.

Agreement. The IEP meeting serves as an opportunity for the charter school and the family to come to agreement about the services expected for the student. It provides a yearly opportunity (at the minimum) for the IEP team to sit down and discuss the programming and placement for the student.

Development of IEP Components

In theory, the IEP is to be developed with all team members sitting around in a room and everyone contributing to the process and helping to write statements. Typically, however, a special education teacher is assigned the responsibility of developing a draft IEP that can then be discussed at the IEP meeting. This draft is then the basis for discussions regarding programming and placement for the student. It is very important that this document be viewed as a draft, and that all participants in the IEP process have an opportunity to provide comments and guidance and to suggest changes to the program. In addition, all the components of the IEP, from the draft stage to the final document, should be described in enough detail so that if the student leaves to go to another school, they can understand the services the student has received and why.

The first step in developing an IEP is to review the student's educational, psychological, psychoeducational, and medical evaluations. Evaluations clarify the specifics of the child's disability and the identified needs which require specially designed instruction. Just as there is no single IEP "form" that schools use, there is no mandated or standardized format for evaluation reports. However, it is very important as a part of the development of the IEP to clearly delineate the student's present levels of academic achievement and functional performance (PLAAFP); this will drive the contents of the IEP and will help to clarify the specifics of the program. Without a PLAAFP statement it is impossible to develop an IEP for a student.

Based on the student's needs (not on what supports are currently available within the charter school), the school develops an individualized program. There may be other students in the school who have similar programs, but each must be developed based on the individual student's needs. All IEPs must include measurable annual goals, a statement of the services to be provided, information on how the student's progress will be monitored, and the student's placement (see Table 4.2). It is important to note that special education is a service and not a placement. Before there is a determination of the actual location where a child will receive special education services, the school should identify those services and supports necessary to help the student meet the goals of the IEP.

> **It is important to note that special education is a service and not a placement. Before there is a determination of the actual location where a child will receive special education services, the school should identify those services and supports necessary to help the student meet the goals of the IEP.**

When developing the statement of services to be provided, consider this guiding question: What will the school do in response to the student's demonstrated needs? Consider such elements as special education and related services, general education classroom modifications, supports to enhance the student's participation in the general education grade-level curriculum, program modifications, and assistive technology. All special education services and strategies for responding to the student's needs must be research- and evidence-based.

As noted in Table 4.2, IDEA directs schools to educate students with disabilities alongside their typically developing peers to the maximum extent appropriate. The *least restrictive environment* is the educational setting in which a student will be challenged to grow, but not experience failure. If the school will be providing special education services to a student in a setting or settings other than the general education classroom, the IEP must explain why this placement is necessary. As with all services provided to students with disabilities, this determination must be based on the student's individual needs and not the convenience of the school or availability of services.

Student IEPs also include projected dates of services to be provided, so that both educational staff and the student's family understand when (and the duration of) and where the services will be implemented. Although IDEA does not specifically address timelines for implementation, most states have developed guidelines on the number of days after an IEP is written that it must take effect. In general, IEPs must be initiated as soon as possible after development.

TABLE 4.2

Development of IEP Components

IEP COMPONENT	CONSIDERATIONS
Measurable annual goals	The goals for the student should be tied directly to the needs as demonstrated and documented in the evaluation of the student. What can be reasonably expected for the student to achieve within the next year? Consider the child's current level of functioning and the grade-level curriculum, and tie this to the development expected for the child over the next year. This is a projected goal which can be changed or modified based on the student's performance.
Special education services to be provided	Considering the goals that are developed for the student, determine the special education services that will be necessary to help the student to master those goals. This is an individual determination for the child, and again is based on the needs of the child and not on what is available within the charter school to address those special education needs. Includes related services, if any are needed.
Progress monitoring	The school must identify how the specified special education services will be monitored for effectiveness. Specifically, the school needs to assess the student's progress toward each goal and objective, and evaluate the effectiveness of the services being delivered. Writing strong, measurable goals will facilitate progress monitoring. In addition, reports of progress on all IEP goals and objectives must be provided to students' families on a regular basis so they are kept informed about programming for their children.
Participation in state assessments	Nearly all students who receive special education services are expected to undergo the same assessments as their typically developing peers, and their academic progress is measured in large part against the performance of all students on mandated state assessments. Students' IEPs must address participation in state assessments; that is, specify one of the following: • The student will take the general assessment. • The student will take the general assessment with appropriate accommodations. (If this is the case, describe the accommodations required by the student.)

TABLE 4.2 *(continued)*

	• The student will take an alternate assessment; state which one. (If this is the case, explain why the student will not be participating in the general assessment and why an alternate assessment is required.)
	• The student will be taking a test based on modified achievement standards. (If this is the case, the IEP must include a discussion of the reason for this choice.)
Placement and LRE	It is important to note that special education is a service and not a placement. A key concept of special education is that of least restrictive environment (LRE). It is the intent of the law that all students with disabilities should be educated to the greatest extent possible alongside their typically developing peers. Thus, the last component in developing a student's IEP is to determine in what settings the delivery of special education services will take place. All students should participate as much as possible in both the academic programming and extracurricular activities of the school but this may not always be possible. The charter school may have to consider placing the student in a more restrictive placement, but placement must be one based on the student's immediate, individual needs.

Developing High-Quality IEPs

As previously noted, there is no single form or format for a student's IEP—and similarly, there is no single set of guidelines for developing high-quality IEPs. There are, however, best practices surrounding identifying students' needs, writing measurable goals, working collaboratively with families and other staff, and collecting data to monitor student progress. Figure 4.2 illustrates the difference between preparing merely adequate IEPs and those that may be highly effective. This figure can be used to provide special education staff with guidance for developing and effectively implementing IEPs, and also provides a tool both to evaluate staff performance and provide insight into areas that need to be developed.

FIGURE 4.2

Adequate Versus Highly Effective IEP Design

COMPETENCY	ADEQUATE	HIGHLY EFFECTIVE
IEP DEVELOPMENT		
Uses recent and relevant academic and social data to plan and draft IEP.	Uses prior assessment and observation data to identify student strengths and weaknesses, present level of performance, and goals.	In addition to fulfilling the adequate criteria at left, • collects and collates new data and observations from relevant school staff. • requests and incorporates parent/student feedback based on current and future goals.
Sets ambitious and measurable achievement goals.	Develops annual goals that are measurable, aligned to content standards, and includes benchmarks to help monitor learning and inform interventions throughout the year.	In addition to fulfilling the adequate criteria at left, • sets high expectations and plans ambitious annual goals.
IEP MEETING		
Is well prepared for IEP meeting.	Organizes logistical details relating to the IEP meeting (location, scheduling, appropriate advance notification to attendees); provides a copy of Procedural Safeguards to family/student at the meeting.	In addition to fulfilling the adequate criteria at left, • is prepared with a draft version of the IEP at the meeting. • provides a copy of Procedural Safeguards to family/student in advance of the meeting.
Communicates information clearly.	• Delivers information that is factually correct. • Explanations are clear, concise, and well-organized. • Restates and rephrases information in multiple ways, to increase family and student understanding. • Encourages family/student participation.	In addition to fulfilling the adequate criteria at left, • fully explains concepts in as direct and efficient a manner as possible, still achieving family/student understanding and using a positive tone. • conference sparks student or family interest in school and learning.

FIGURE 4.2 (continued)

COMPETENCY	ADEQUATE	HIGHLY EFFECTIVE

PROGRESS MONITORING

COMPETENCY	ADEQUATE	HIGHLY EFFECTIVE
Goals respond to the student's current level of functioning	• Writes strong, measurable goals; this actually happens during IEP development but is important when it comes to progress monitoring. • Reports of progress on all IEP goals and objectives are provided to students' families on a regular basis so they are kept informed about programming for their children. • Identifies timeline for progress monitoring and reporting.	Ideally, all charter schools would have as much money as needed to provide services for students with disabilities to ensure that all students make progress toward grade-level academic standards. The reality is, however, that it is very difficult to predict the true costs of providing an appropriate education, and most charter schools do not have the same range of resources as traditional public schools and school districts to meet students' needs.

Incorporates progress monitoring data	• Strives to use information from student progress monitoring when updating/reevaluating decisions about programming and placement. This effort not only helps students but also helps teachers to plan instruction.
	• Monitoring the progress of students who receive special education services also guides the school in refining the services it provides.
		• Monitors student progress frequently, at least monthly, and more frequently when trying to determine how students are responding to interventions.
		• Graphs the student's progress and compares it to expected progress and to the rates of others. Effective progress monitoring offers various additional benefits:
		  • Teachers are more aware of students' progress in the curriculum and meeting grade-level expectations.
		  • Teachers use data to make informed instructional decisions.
		  • Teachers can communicate more easily and accurately with families regarding students' progress, strengths, and challenges.
		  • Teachers and other school staff can use the information to determine whether to refer a student for referral for additional services.
		  • Teachers can provide enrichment for students who have already mastered grade-level curriculum.

FIGURE 4.2 *(continued)*

COMPETENCY	ADEQUATE	HIGHLY EFFECTIVE
PROGRESS MONITORING *(continued)*		
Uses data for decision making	• Describes how the student's progress toward meeting the annual goals will be measured; covers timing of periodic progress reports (e.g., at same time as academic report cards for other students). • Identifies how the specified special education services will be monitored for effectiveness. Specifically, the school needs to assess the student's progress toward each goal and objective, and evaluate the effectiveness of the services being delivered.	To be effective, progress monitoring should be frequent but relatively short and easy to administer. Teachers should collect and graph data, and these data should be used to help make informed decisions.
Collects data from a variety of resources	• Compiles/organizes data on progress toward IEP goals—in addition to notes and comments from teachers and others working with the child—in such a way that it can be used for establishing a need for continued special education services. • Progress monitoring of programs and services based on the plans and goals developed is just as important at the systemic level as it is for assessing students' progress toward their IEP goals.	• Potential behavioral strategy: put student on a daily/weekly progress report. • Continuous student monitoring enables a school to track the number of times a student requires individualized instruction, which could potentially be an important determining factor about whether the student needs more help via intensive instruction.

Note. Adapted with permission from Goodwill Education Initiatives of Central Indiana's internal Case Conference assessment rubric.

Transition IEPs

As part of the services they provide to students with disabilities, charter schools need to prepare students for the transition to life after high school. The requirement to include the student in transition planning at age 16 (if not earlier) stemmed from concerns regarding postsecondary outcomes for students with disabilities. The IEP team must develop transition goals based on the individual student's postschool plans and support the student in achieving progress toward those plans in the areas of training, education, employment, and as appropriate, independent living skills. Like all IEP goals, transition goals should be appropriate, measurable, and based on age-appropriate assessments.

Transition services provided to the student need to be directly linked to these goals. In addition, transition services need to include educating the student in the rights of the age of majority under state law.

Like traditional public schools, charter schools do not need to be able to provide all transition support services in-house, and may be able to draw on services available from other networked schools or in the community. Building a community team (see Mazzotti & Rowe, 2015; Noonan, 2014) enhances and strengthens a charter school's relationships and partnerships, and also can improve the services provided.

IEPs for Students With Behavioral Disorders

When developing an IEP, the team needs to consider whether and how the student's behavior affects other students, so "in the case of a child whose behavior impedes the child's learning or that of others, consider the use of positive behavioral interventions and supports, and other strategies, to address that behavior" (20 U.S.C. § 1414[d][3][B][I]).

When developing an IEP that includes behavioral interventions, the charter school needs to address how the special education services provided will respond to the student's needs. In developing such a statement and plan for support, conduct an assessment of the behavior. Behavioral assessments generally consider the environment in which the behavior occurs, antecedents (events or activities immediately preceding the behavior), and consequences (events or actions in response to the behavior). The data collected as part of the behavioral assessment provide insight into the function of the student's behavior, which in turn provides guidance in developing a plan (see Baditoi, 2010) to reduce problem behavior and increase socially acceptable behaviors.

One of the most difficult responsibilities of a charter school administrator is how to effectively discipline students with disabilities. There are important regulations, rules, and procedures regarding the discipline of students with disabilities that do not exist for the general student population. This—coupled with the increasing demands for safe schools and zero tolerance for violations of drugs, alcohol, and weapons—can create an uneasy mix for both special and general educators. The charter school administrator must ensure all staff understand the steps necessary for dealing with disciplining students with disabilities.

Federal law requires schools to conduct a *manifestation determination review* when a student with a disability has "violated any rule or code of conduct" that applies to all students in the school (34 C.F.R. §300.523). That is, the school administrator needs to assess whether there is a relationship between the student's disability "and the behavior subject to the disciplinary action" (34 C.F.R. §300.523[a][2]). The IDEA regulations delineate the processes schools must follow in conducting such a review; see Appendix C for a flowchart summarizing the overall process and considerations (see Bateman, 2014, pp. 114–119, for a more in-depth discussion of the process).

The emphasis on discipline for students with disabilities has to be positive in nature. Some schools incorporate systems of positive reinforcement for group or individual demonstration of desirable behavior. However, even if that is all that is done, the true nature of dealing with behavior problems can still be incomplete. Every school should have a comprehensive support system that helps to shape appropriate behaviors and also has embedded the necessary steps and strategies for when a true crisis emerges. This system should include how to document potential problems, strategies used to address the problem, and how these behavior management strategies are incorporated into a student's IEP or behavior management plan.

Case Study: Tough Love in DC

District of Columbia Public Charter School Board
Washington, DC

Since January of 2012, Naomi Rubin DeVeaux has served as deputy director of the District of Columbia Public Charter School Board (DC PCSB). In November of 2015, DC PCSB (along with other education agencies) released the third annual citywide discipline equity reports—and the level of data publicly released was unprecedented. DeVeaux stressed that "Our goal with displaying school's suspension and expulsion data was to be transparent and not punitive. When we released our school's discipline data, we were unapologetic about our approach. It's a conversation that needed to happen."

This level of transparency was needed, DeVeaux believed, to fully understand and answer critical questions about how successfully schools were closing the achievement gap between Black and White students, and between low-income and more affluent students; whether children of color were being suspended at higher rates than were White students; and how well schools were serving students with disabilities. DeVeaux has stated that "schools need space to be able to be honest and retool when things are not working. They also may need help finding effective behavior and discipline models that align with the vision and missions of their school."

Throughout the process, DeVeaux and DC PCSB learned some important lessons about how to reduce expulsion and suspension rates, including

- Recognize that schools need time and support to implement change. Rather than set hard targets, seek improvement over time.

- Address concerns with school board members and school leaders together.

- Recognize that schools need to be able to define and defend their discipline models and their data.

- Include suspensions and midyear withdrawal rates when evaluating a school's request to expand or renew its charter.

- Annually analyze expulsions, suspensions, midyear withdrawals, and attendance rates, and publish the data. If the school is part of a collaborative, make the data available to all schools in real time, comparing their data to sectorwide averages for all students and across subgroups.

- Seek the support of consultants to help develop tools that schools can use to evaluate their delivery of special education services.

- For school-specific discipline plans, ensure that consequences and expectations are developmentally appropriate.

- Invest in mental health services onsite to help address many of the root causes of discipline issues.

Related Services

In an IEP, the phrase "related services" refers to additional support intended to assist students with disabilities in benefiting from special education services. Related services include transportation, speech-language and audiology services, interpreting services, psychological services, physical and occupational therapy, recreation, counseling, orientation and mobility services, and medical services. These services may be provided by specialists, school nurses, social workers, or other professionals. If a child needs a particular related service in order to benefit from special education, the related service professional should be involved in developing the IEP.

Section 504 Plans

Some students with disabilities are not eligible for special education and related services; instead, they may receive accommodations and support via a Section 504 plan (see Chapter 2 for an overview). Like IEPs, Section 504 plans can help students with learning and attention issues to participate in and gain more from the general education curriculum. Students with 504 plans typically spend the entire school day in a general education classroom, and the responsibility for ensuring they receive appropriate accommodations rests on the general education classroom teacher. In developing Section 504 plans, charter schools should collect documentation of the student's disability (e.g., medical diagnosis), evaluation results (if the school recently evaluated the student for special education services, or if supplied by the family), observations from parents and teachers, and the student's academic record. Like an IEP, a 504 plan can include specialized instruction in a general education classroom setting. Unlike IEPs, 504 plans do not include annual goals.

As with IEPs, there is no standard form to develop Section 504 plans, and every state offers different guidelines. However, there are certain elements 504 plans should include, all tailored to a student's individual needs:

- The specific accommodations, supports, or services to be provided (see Table 4.3).

- An identification of who in the school will provide the services.

- The name of the person responsible for ensuring the Section 504 plan is implemented.

TABLE 4.3

Section 504 Plan Possible Accommodations

AREA OF ACCOMMODATION	EXAMPLES
Environmental strategies	Provide a structured learning environment.
	Provide preferential seating.
	Alter location of classroom supplies for easier access.
	Consider use of nonacademic times, such as recess or lunch (e.g., when placement within an alternate student group is desired, or when a student resists being pulled out of class).
Organizational strategies	Model organizational systems.
	Check student's recording of assignments.
	Change time expectations for assignments.
	Provide clues to indicate beginning and ending times.
Behavioral strategies	Implement behavioral contracts.
	Confer with the student's parent.
	Establish a home and school communication system.
	Post rules and consequences for classroom behavior.
	Report to student's family on daily/weekly progress.
	Reinforce self-monitoring and self-recording of behaviors.
Presentation strategies	Record lessons so the student can listen to them more than once.
	Highlight main ideas and supporting details in the book.
	Vary the method of lesson presentation.

Note. An *accommodation* is a change in the course, standard, location, timing, scheduling, expectations, or student response that provides access for a student with a disability to participate in a course or test, and which does not fundamentally alter or lower the standard or expectation of the content (Bateman & Cline, 2016b).

CHAPTER CAPSTONE

More Than Compliance Documents

Students with disabilities may be eligible to receive special education and related services via an IEP. Other students with disabilities who are not eligible for special education services but nonetheless require accommodations to access school functions and curricula require a Section 504 plan. Both IEPs and 504 plans are binding; charter schools are required to develop and implement plans appropriate to a student's individual needs. Again, IEP and Section 504 plans are more than paperwork compliance documents; they guide the programming and accommodations provided for students with disabilities.

Writing and implementing strong IEPs—based on data, delineating clear goals, and providing a means of monitoring progress—is essential to ensuring that students receive the support they need, and to establishing long-term relationships. Making sure that data is confidential and procedures are transparent helps to promote communication among and commitment from all parties. The individualization of a student's IEP is the foundation of providing special education services; each student's IEP must be based on that child's individual needs, strengths, and goals.

CHAPTER 5

Starting Up and Closing Down

With Karega Rausch, Kristin Hines, and Brandon Brown

Across the United States, charter schools are figuring out what special education will "look like" in their distinctive educational settings, delivery models, and curricula. As discussed in Chapter 1, uniqueness and individuality are characteristics that are embraced by both charter schools and special education on a very basic level. Special education teachers are versed in multiple methodologies and pedagogies, continually filling their "teaching tool kits" with a variety of strategies, interventions, and techniques in hopes of finding something there that works for each individual student. Charter schools embody this same innovative and problem-solving spirit but from a more systemic perspective. Charter schools are also trying something different, as entire schools and for a large number of students. Sometimes charter schools succeed, and sometimes they fail.

One of the most striking aspects of the charter school movement is school closure. Authorizers hold charter schools accountable for performance or schools are closed. Charters can be revoked if schools do not live up to their agreement. The closure of charter schools presents a challenge for the national charter school movement because school closure is a new experience for many. The public is used to thinking of schools as fixed entities in a community; school closure is considered shocking and disruptive. Prominent members of the charter movement have supported the use of accountability as a fundamental way to ensure the success of charter schools. The idea of opening a new business seems just as normal to most people as a going out of business sale. But the idea of opening a new public school or closing one has been unheard of until recent years.

How charters choose to navigate special education issues could prove to be a pivotal question in the future success of the movement. Future predictions of population growth depict continually climbing numbers of students identified as having some kind of disability (Samuels, 2016). In early 2016, the Centers for Disease Control and Prevention reported that more than one in seven children in the United States had a mental, behavioral, or developmental disorder (Bitsko et al., 2016). Data like these are hard to ignore and paint a vivid picture of the future services that all public educational environments will need to provide.

Openings and closings of public charter schools are two such opportunities that now present themselves on a regular basis. As discussed in Chapter 1, the charter school movement offers special education the opportunity to examine currently accepted and established practices, policies, and procedures under new circumstances and in new contexts. Historically, the design of individual public schools has not been based on a re-search-based pedagogical model. Educators, communities, and students with disabilities and their families are now finding themselves in new situations. Accordingly, school-lev-el accountability and high expectations may not only allow but also drive individual charter schools to incorporate innovative educational practices. It can take some time for a charter school to get up and running smoothly. Constructive and critical reflection on these new models is essential to avoid facing closures.

Starting Up: Considerations When Opening a Charter School

Special education should be considered a foundational piece in the establishment of every charter school. Special education cuts across several areas that are vital to the overall health of the organization. What may begin as considerations relating to physical space and access influences hiring and retention of highly qualified special and general education teachers, leaders, and support staff. Such considerations extend to a school's professional development and the accessibility of the school's mission, vision, and curriculum.

As mentioned in Chapter 3, developing an inclusive climate and a positive learning environment that perceives students as "at-potential" benefits all students. This type of philosophy is also in line with the Council for Exceptional Children's (CEC) Code of Ethics, which encourages educators to

- Maintain challenging expectations for students with disabilities, in order to promote the highest learning outcomes.
- Maintain a high level of professional competence and integrity.

> **Developing an inclusive climate and a positive learning environment that perceives students as "at-potential" benefits all students.**

- Promote meaningful and inclusive participation of students with disabilities in their schools and communities.
- Work collaboratively to provide educational services.
- Develop relationships with families.
- Incorporate evidence-based strategies into educational practice.
- Advocate for improved learning outcomes for students. (CEC, 2016, pp. 7–8)

CEC's standards for professional practice *(What Every Special Educator Must Know;* 2016) can help support decision making on a more detailed and logistical level, help-ing to ensure that a school's staffing, policies, and services meet the requirements of the field and the law. The set of standards is divided into nine subcategories: teaching and assessment, professional credentials and employment, professional development, professional colleagues, paraprofessionals, parents and families, research, case management, and non-educational support. For each of these subcategories, there are specific types of activities that special education professionals must be prepared to undertake; the CEC standards also set a level of performance that they should strive to achieve. In addition, the delineated knowledge and skill sets in CEC's *What Every Special Educator Must Know* (2016) can serve to support evaluation of candidate qualifications for meeting the needs of students with different disabilities and the requirements of specific administrative roles.

Adopting CEC's standards as part of program development is a valuable way to ensure clarity and quality of services in a charter application. In some cases, application of the standards may indicate that the school will be working toward these standards in future decision making for resource allocation, staff evaluation and goal setting, and community engagement and outreach efforts, as well as relationship building with all stakeholders. The National Charter School Resource Center's *Special Education Start-Up and Implementation Tools* (2012), developed in cooperation with the National Association of State Directors of Special Education (NASDSE), can be downloaded for free and suggests a wide variety of resources for charter schools administrators seeking to establish high-quality special education services. Using high-quality standards and resources from organizations like CEC and NASDSE is essential to designing effective special education services and programming.

The Role of Authorizers

A charter school authorizer is responsible for deciding who should start a new charter school, setting performance expectations, overseeing school performance, and deciding who should continue to operate charter schools (National Association of Charter School Authorizers [NACSA], 2015b). Authorizers are creations of state policy and thus differ somewhat in their roles and responsibilities across states. Generally, however, authorizers

- Establish and execute application processes to approve or deny charter school applications.
- Execute a performance-based contract (i.e., the charter) that defines the academic, operational, and financial performance expectations for a charter school, as well as compliance responsibilities to federal and state law.
- Create and implement an oversight system to monitor performance and fidelity to terms of the charter.
- Make determinations to renew, not renew, or revoke a school's charter (Hassel & Vergari, 1999; NACSA, 2015a; Vergari, 2000).

TABLE 5.1

Charter School Authorizing Agencies

AGENCY	EXPLANATION
Local education agencies (LEAs)	Traditional school districts act as the LEA for the majority of charter schools in the United States.
State education agencies (SEAs)	In 18 states, individual state departments of education (SEAs) authorize charter schools.
Higher education institutions (HEIs)	Forty-five colleges and universities act as authorizers across the United States.
Not-for-profit organizations (NFPs)	There are 17 NFPs acting in an authorizing role nationally.
Non-educational governmental municipalities (NEGs)	Only three NEGs serve as authorizers, making mayors or municipalities the smallest group of charter school authorizers.
Independent chartering boards (ICBs)	There are 17 statewide entities created exclusively for the purpose of charter school authorizing.

As authorizers serve both a gatekeeping and accountability function, they are a lynchpin for the quality of charter schools across the United States, including how well charter schools serve students with disabilities.

NACSA's annual surveys of charter school authorizers indicate that authorizers vary tremendously in type and number of school they oversee. Authorizers are typically categorized into six groups (see Table 5.1; NACSA, 2015b). Among the 1,053 authorizers across 42 states and the District of Columbia in the 2013–2014 school year, more than 90% were school districts (NACSA, 2015b). The number of schools overseen by authorizers also varies widely: More than half of all authorizers oversee just a single charter school, and 80% of authorizers oversee fewer than five schools. In contrast, the nation's largest authorizer, the Texas Education Agency, oversees 644 charter schools.

As is inherent to the charter school movement, accountability and high expectations are principles that also apply to charter school authorizers. The National Alliance for Public Charter Schools (2009) has advocated for an authorizer system that is reflective of the school-level accountability system in place for charter schools. According to this position, authorizers should adhere to national standards, be rigorously assessed prior to selection and annually report on their own and charter school performance. Authorizers who do not meet these standards (like the charter schools they authorize) would be subject to termination.

NACSA has also weighed in on the issue of authorizer accountability, recommending establishing authorizer standards, evaluating authorizers in light of these standards, requiring annual reports on school performance, and providing sanctions for failing authorizers. NACSA's Principles & Standards for Quality Charter School Authorizing (2015a) were created to maintain high standards for schools, uphold school autonomy, and protect student and public interests.

The standards are differentiated developmentally, based on the experience of the authorizer. The first, fundamental layer of authorizing standards are called Essential Standards. Authorizers who have mastered implementing these practices are encouraged to work toward implementing Advanced Standards.

Given the powerful role charter school authorizers play and the historic lack of support they have received in the area of special education, the National Center for Special Education in Charter Schools (NCSECS) recently developed a three-phase rubric for charter school authorizers to improve their capacity to support development and maintenance of high quality special education programs (Rhim & O'Neill, 2012; see Appendix). The rubric focuses on three phases of the charter authorizing process: application and replication, operations and oversight, and renewal and reauthorization. The rubric is intended to help authorizers assess an applicant's ability to provide high-quality special education programs, ensure transparency throughout the authorizing process, provide a framework for charter schools' services for students with disabilities, and enable assessment of individual charter school practices.

••

Case Study: Coming Together in California

Magnolia Public Schools
California

California is home to some of the largest school systems in the United States. The state's public schools special education services are overseen by regional Special Education Local Plan Areas (SELPAs). Since the establishment of SELPAs in 1977, educational policy has changed and school structures have evolved; charter schools in California today work with local SELPAs to implement special education services. Although originally charters were bound to their traditional district's SELPA, each now has the power to choose its SELPA and be able to leave a SELPA that is not meeting its needs.

Magnolia Public Schools (MPS) was formed in 2002 and serves the Los Angeles, Orange County, San Diego, and Silicon Valley areas, working with three SELPAs to provide special education services to students with disabilities across 11 different schools. MPS includes four middle schools, one elementary school, and six middle/high schools serving Grades 6 to 8. According to CEO and Superintendent Caprice Young,

Collaboration is what makes it happen. Thankfully, we are seeing that the next generation of educators are peacemakers and innovators. Our director of student services, Kelly Hourigan, and the LA Unified School District's SELPA director, Sydney Quon, in particular are doing inspiring work together every day.

Hourigan and Quon both considered special education a uniting fabric of their educational community. Hourigan noted that "charters have the freedom to open the door to innovation. Sydney's leadership has enabled us to try new things in special education and build a sense of community among the LA charters."

According to Quon, who serves as the director of special education for all charter schools within the LA Unified School District, this work is not for everyone and is dependent on relationship building. "I wasn't from here," she said. "I wasn't part of the really hard conversations of the past, so I was able to come in as a neutral party and act as a negotiator. I spent the first year just building relationships with everyone."

Young, Hourigan, and Quon have learned many valuable lessons over the course of their time navigating the relationship between Magnolia Public School and LA Unified's SELPA, such as

- Shared leadership is critical. Quon is an LA Unified employee, but her position is funded by the charters, and the charter schools evaluate her. This professional sharing of the position set the stage for trust building—and the importance of trust and transparency cannot be overstated.

- Talk money last. Money is always a tough conversation, and in a situation where there are lots of tough issues to work through, tackle the issues that are most likely to bring people together first as a way to build relationships and shared ownership of the ideas and solutions.

- Host common meetings and build a sense of community among your schools. Clear and timely communication ensures a smooth process.

- Share models of best practice across all school structures. Take groups from both charters and traditional public schools to observe the best in each other and begin sharing those ideas across schools.

We Got Our Charter! Now What?

Maintaining Strong Special Education Programming

Once an authorizer has approved a charter application and awarded the charter, a school leader must begin actually building the school. In special education terms, that means the school leader must first define the school's LEA status. Most charter schools currently fall within one of two categories: constituting their own LEA or being part of an existing LEA. As discussed in Chapter 4, a charter school that is considered its own

LEA under state law is solely responsible for all special education requirements, just as is any other LEA in that state. A charter school that is part of an existing LEA carries responsibility that has been mutually agreed upon, typically via a contract, at the level of a school within that LEA. Typically, the LEA retains most or all of the responsibility for special education in the charter school. It is important that the charter school board and the authorizer understand the expectations of both designations, understand which option is available based on state law, and have a shared understanding of the responsibilities of the individual charter school.

Once a school has established its LEA designation, attention turns to the details of fleshing out the plan for the school, from building choices to staffing to student recruitment. This process includes many individual elements (see Table 5.2), and each should incorporate best practices in providing special education services. Once basic policies and procedures have been established, it is important to track their effectiveness as they are implemented in the day-to-day school environment.

Similarly, a school may be wise to compile student records on an annual or semi-annual basis using a template such as a summary of performance (see Sopko, 2008; Wrightslaw, 2010), a transition document public schools are required to provide students graduating or aging out of that educational setting. Such record compilation will greatly aid in the transfer of a student who leaves the school for any reason and, as discussed in the next section, the navigation of school closure should it occur.

As stated previously, it can take a charter school a while to get up and running smoothly. The importance of constructive and critical reflection during this time cannot be overemphasized. Charter schools should develop plans and goals for the first 5 years of a program's existence. These plans and goals should be specifically tied to strategic planning efforts and curriculum development and delivery, as well as staff evaluations and student achievement. At times, a charter school authorizer will require goals for the length of the charter—which may be longer than 5 years. Progress monitoring of programs and services based on the plans and goals developed is just as important at the systemic level as it is for assessing students' progress toward their IEP goals. It is important to help staff celebrate when programmatic goals have been met, and also to take time to fully understand when goals are not met and adjust accordingly.

Once the program is up and running, a charter school should reach out to other schools in the same region to develop partnerships and collaborations. Many times, sharing services like transportation, psychological evaluation services, and occupational and physical therapies can be ways to begin building productive relationships among schools, providing a community focused on offering high quality services for students with disabilities. Schools can also encourage their staff to reach out to their professional counterparts to share ideas and realities. Identifying the issues with special education in a region can be key in an individual school's being able to ensure that its students are getting the best services it can offer.

TABLE 5.2

Pre-Opening Activities

ACTIVITY	HINTS AND TIPS
Lottery procedures and policies	• Maintain appropriate weights across demographics, if and where allowed by laws governing open enrollment. • Publicly publish dates and timelines in advance according to local and federal regulations.
Marketing/student recruitment plan	• What curricular products or overarching program will the school use? • Identify the target audience or student demographics, and the objective for the target audience. • Establish a timeline and budget. • Measure and evaluate the return on marketing investment.
Staffing plan[a]	• Identify the role and responsibility of the primary staff member responsible for overseeing special education service delivery (e.g., Special Education Coordinator, Special Education Director, Special Education Manager). • Identify the special education administrator. • Include in staffing plans both general and special education teachers (and possible co-teaching models). • Identify the role of permanent paraprofessional and other supporting staff members (e.g., speech–language, counselors).
Related service providers and external vendors[a]	• Identify resources in LEA and community (e.g., health-related services, speech–language services, transportation). • Develop preliminary contract materials. • Identify legal counsel.
Internal processes and procedures	• Draft policy and procedure manuals that align with mission and vision. • Identify schoolwide positive behavior supports to be used. • Identify process for evaluating staff.
Child Find procedures and policies[b]	• Establish methods for identifying and locating students with exceptionalities. • Identify base level of services for all students and response-to-intervention processes. • Establish internal evaluation and assessment practices.
Documentation and data systems	• Create IEP forms and systems (e.g., file checklists, procedure diagrams) procedure diagrams). • Establish service delivery schedule. • Identify timeline for progress monitoring and reporting.

Note. LEA = local education agency; IEP = individualized education program.
[a] See Chapter 3. [b] See Chapter 2.

Starting special education programs from scratch may seem to be a daunting task. At many existing charter schools, special education services have emerged based on available funding, authorizer requirements, and student need. Schools that are starting up have an opportunity to structure their staffing and support systems to incorporate responding to the needs of students with disabilities and their obligations under federal and state law.

Closing Down: Considerations for Closing a Charter School

A major component of the charter school movement is accountability and experimentation with innovative educational practices. This also means that charter schools can close. The closing of a school is a fairly new experience for a public who has seen very few schools closed prior to the charter movement. The National Association of Charter School Authorizers has laid out procedures for closing a failing charter school (Shaw, 2011; Wechtenhiser, Wade, & Lin, 2010; see Figure 5.1).

FIGURE 5.1

Closing Down

STRATEGIC PLANNING
- Meet with authorizer.
- Establish transition/closing team, assign responsibilities.
- Clarify financial reporting requirements.

DEVELOP CLOSURE PLAN
- Set deadlines for activities, schedule notifications.
- Arrange for handling of student and corporate records.
- Determine treatment of debtors, creditors, assets.
- Corporate activities (closing bank accounts, terminating staff, final tax payments).

DEVELOP COMMUNICATION PLAN
- Plan notification to stakeholders, talking points. for different constituencies.
- Write press release.
- Set up meetings with families, staff, community.

Timing the announcement of a planned school closure is a delicate thing. There is tension between giving parents the time to make choices for the upcoming year and providing students with a high-quality education for the remainder of the current school year. If the announcement is made too early, schools can lose staff and students prematurely, or a negative climate can take hold for the remainder of the year. If the announcement is made too late, families and students may not have adequate time to pick a satisfactory new school.

It is important to keep in mind that students with IEPs and their families have a unique set of needs when navigating a school closure. Although all families will encounter stress when a school closes, families of students with disabilities have additional concerns: finding a new appropriate placement, ensuring that students' IEPs and supporting records are complete, and the emotional burden surrounding what can be a very challenging transition.

Schools and authorizers must ensure that students with IEPs do not have a lapse in services based on a school closing. Schools must ensure that student records—including IEPs, psychological evaluations, 504 plans, and medical records—are all handled according to the Individuals With Disabilities Education Act (IDEA), the Family Educational Rights and Privacy Act (FERPA), and the Health Insurance Portability and Accountability Act (HIPAA) regulations regarding confidentiality and timelines for transfer. To facilitate this process, schools may be wise to compile student records on an annual or semi-annual basis using a template such as a summary of performance (see Sopko, 2008; Wrightslaw, 2010), a transition document public schools are required to provide students graduating or aging out of that educational setting.

In the event of a closure, students and families need time to adjust and mourn the loss of their previous school. It is also important to make sure students and families are able to transition smoothly into the new school's culture and climate. Many students with disabilities thrive on stability and consistency, so it is important that the authorizer and the new school communicate often; following up throughout the year can help ensure a student's transition is successful.

BOOK CAPSTONE

Intentional Innovation

The charter school movement has presented a variety of new scenarios within the educational ecosystem. Charter schools have an unprecedented amount of autonomy and accountability, so their influence on the larger field cannot be ignored. In many ways, charter schools present an opportunity to innovate special education practice in ways we have yet to imagine. For the first time, the opportunity exists to create mission-driven schools that include students with disabilities by design rather than as an add-on. Charters can cultivate special education infrastructures, innovate service provision models, and conduct research to track effectiveness and financial sustainability.

These opportunities come with inherent challenges. In order to realize these opportunities, charters must figure out how to grow in their technical knowledge and capacity, while also addressing the realities of offering a full continuum of services without the economies of scale that exist in traditional public schools. Students with IEPs deserve just as many high quality educational options as their typically developing peers. For charters to be able to have a lasting and authentic effect, they must figure out how to solve problems that have yet to be solved. If charters fail to find new ways to support students who have struggled in traditional public schools, then what does the movement offer that was not already present? Can they claim to be any different than the schools that have come before them?

References

Ahearn, E. (1999, March). *Charter schools and special education: A report on state policies.* Alexandria, VA: National Association of State Directors of Special Education. Retrieved from http://www.cesa7.org/sped/discoveridea/topdocs/spec_ed_policies.htm

Ahearn, E. (2010, April). *Financing special education: State funding formulas.* Washington, DC: National Association of State Directors of Special Education. Retrieved from http://nasdse.org/DesktopModules/DNNspot-Store/ProductFiles/82_dce66976-08dd-4cdd-abbd-1397e973c81a.pdf

American Society for Testing and Materials. (2011). *ASTM F1487-11, Standard consumer safety performance specification for playground equipment for public use.* West Conshohocken, PA: Author.

Baditoi, B., & Brott, P. (2014). *What school counselors need to know about special education and students with disabilities* (Rev. ed.). Arlington, VA: Council for Exceptional Children.

Baditoi, B. E. (2010). *When behavior makes learning hard: Positive steps for changing student behavior.* Arlington, VA: Council for Exceptional Children

Baltimore City Public Schools. (2012). *After nearly three decades, City schools fully emerges from Vaughn G. litigation* [Press release]. Retrieved from http://www.clearinghouse.net/chDocs/public/ED-MD-0001-0004.pdf

Bateman, B. D., & Herr, C. M. (2006). *Writing measureable IEP goals and objectives.* Verona, WI: IEP Resources.

Bateman, D. F., & Bateman, C. F. (2014). *A principal's guide to special education* (3rd ed.). Arlington, VA: Council for Exceptional Children.

Bateman, D. F., & Cline, J. L (2016a). *Effective and efficient management of resources* (CASE Special Education Leadership Monograph Series). Warner Robins, GA: Council of Administrators of Special Education.

Bateman, D. F., & Cline, J. L. (2016b). *A teacher's guide to special education.* Alexandria, VA: Association for Supervision & Curriculum Development.

Beigh, D. (2012, June 16). Indiana school voucher program doubling to 15,000 in 2012-13. *Indiana Economic Digest.* Retrieved from http://indianaeconomicdigest.com/main.asp?SectionID=31&SubSectionID=77&ArticleID=65398

Bitsko, R. H., Holbrook, J. R., Robinson, L. R., Kaminski, J. W., Ghandour, R., Smith, C., & Peacock, G. (2016). Health care, family, and community factors associated with mental, behavioral, and developmental disorders in early childhood—United States, 2011–2012. *Morbidity and Mortality Weekly Report (MMWR).* doi:10.15585/mmwr.mm6509a1

Bogdan, W. K. (2011). *Trends and issues affecting special education and the provision of special education services.* Warner Robins, GA: Council for Administrators of Special Education.

Boundy, K. B. (2012). *Charter schools and students with disabilities: Preliminary analysis of legal issues and areas of concern.* Towson, MD: Council of Parent Attorneys and Advocates.

Brown v. Board of Education. 347 U.S. 483. (1954)

Budde, R. (1988). *Education by charter: Restructuring school districts. Key to long-term continuing improvement in American education.* Waltham, MA: Regional Educational Laboratory for Educational Improvement of the Northeast & Islands. Retrieved from https://www.edreform.com/wp-content/uploads/2014/12/Education-by-Charter-Restructuring-School-Districts-Ray-Budde.pdf

Budde, R. (1995). *Strengthen school-based management by chartering all schools: A three-year, policy-based strategy for creating autonomous public schools within restructured school districts.* Waltham, MA: Regional Educational Laboratory for Educational Improvement of the Northeast & Islands.

Budde, R. (1996). The evolution of the charter concept. *Phi Delta Kappan, 78*(1), 72–73. Retrieved from http://www.worldcat.org/oclc/427183047

Burlington School Committee v. Massachusetts Department of Education, 471 US 359 (1985).

Citizens League. (1988). *Citizens League report. Chartered schools = Choices for educators + quality for all students.* Minneapolis, MN: Author. Retrieved from http://citizensleague.org/wp-content/uploads/2013/05/424.Report.Chartered-Schools-Choices-for-Education-Quality-for-All-Students.pdf

Clinton, W. J. (1998) *Remarks on presenting the Presidential Medal of Freedom.* Santa Barbara, CA: The American Presidency Project. Retrieved from http://www.presidency.ucsb.edu/ws/?pid=55813

Council for Exceptional Children. (2015). *Charter schools.* Retrieved from https://www.cec.sped.org/Policy-and-Advocacy/More-Issues/Charter-Schools

Council for Exceptional Children. (2016). *What every special educator must know: Professional ethics & standards*. Arlington, VA: Author.

Cross, C. (2004). *Political education: National policy comes of age*. New York, NY: Teachers College Press.

Division for Learning Disabilities. (2008). *Thinking about response to intervention and learning disabilities: A teacher's guide*. Arlington, VA: Author.

Duncan, A. (2013, July 2). *Secretary Arne Duncan's remarks to the National Alliance for Public Charter Schools 2013 "Delivering on the Dream" conference*. Cambridge, MA: The Education Innovation Laboratory at Harvard University. Retrieved from http://edlabs.harvard.edu/news/arne-duncan-praises-edlabs-work-napcs-conference

Editorial. (1913, January 27). Schools ask for help with defectives. *The New York Times*. Retrieved from http://query.nytimes.com/gst/abstract.html?res=9502E7D81E3AE633A25754C2A9679C-946296D6CF

Family Educational Rights and Privacy Act of 1974, 20 U.S.C. § 1232g. (2006)

Felch, J., Song, J., & Smith, D. (2010, August 14). Who's teaching L.A.'s kids? *Los Angeles Times*. Retrieved from http://articles.latimes.com/2010/aug/14/local/la-me-teachers-value-20100815

Fiore, T. A., & Cashman, E. R. (1998). *Review of charter school legislation provisions related to students with disabilities*. Washington, DC: U.S. Department of Education. Retrieved from http://eric.ed.gov/?id=ED426511

Fiore, T. A., Warren, S. H., & Cashman, E. R. (1998). *Public charter schools and students with disabilities: Review of existing data*. Washington, DC: U.S. Department of Education, Office of Educational Research and Improvement. Retrieved from http://www.ericdigests.org/2002-2/public.htm

Freedman, M. K., Bisbicos, M. E., Jentz, C. B., & Orenstein, E. (2005, November 29). Special education at 30: Dreams, realities, and possibilities. *Education Week*. Retrieved from http://www.edweek.org/ew/articles/2005/11/30/13freedman.h25.html

Friedman Foundation for Educational Choice. (2016). *The ABCs of school choice: The comprehensive guide to every private school choice program in America*. Indianapolis, IN: Author. Retrieved from http://www.edchoice.org/wp-content/uploads/2016/02/2016-ABCs-WEB-2.pdf

Garda, R. (2012). Culture clash: Special education in charter schools. *North Carolina Law Review*, *90*, 656–718. Retrieved from http://www.public-charters.org/wp-content/uploads/2015/04/Culture-Clash-Special-Education-in-Charter-Schools.pdf

Giovannetti, B., & Opalack, N. (2008). *The special education project: A study of 23 charter schools in the Recovery School District*. Southaven, MS: Educational Support Systems.

Government Accountability Office. (2012). *Charter schools: Additional federal attention needed to help protect access for students with disabilities*. Washington, DC: Author. Retrieved from http://www.gao.gov/assets/600/591435.pdf

Green, P. C., & Mead, J. F. (2004). *Charter schools and the law: Chartering new legal relationships*. Norwood, MA: Christopher-Gordon.

Grimes, D. (2012). *Michigan's transition to a knowledge-based economy: Fifth annual report*. Ann Arbor: Michigan Futures.

Hassel, B. C., & Vergari, S. (1999). Charter-granting agencies: The challenges of oversight in a deregulated system. *Education and Urban Society*, *31*, 406–428.

Hawf, A. (2015, March 30). Special education governance in New Orleans [Web log post]. Center on Reinventing Public Education. Retrieved from http://www.crpe.org/thelens/special-education-governance-new-orleans

Heubert, J. P. (1997). Schools without rules? Charter schools, federal disability law, and the paradoxes of deregulation. *Harvard Civil Rights-Civil Liberties Law Review*, *32*, 301–353.

H.R. 4330: All Students Achieving Through Reform Act of 2009: Hearing Before the Committee on Education and Labor, February 24, 2010, House of Representatives, 111th Cong. (2010).

Individuals With Disabilities Education Act, 20 U. S. C. §§ 1400 et seq. (2006 & Supp. V. 2011)

Johnson, L. B. (1965, January 12). *Special message to the Congress: Toward full educational opportunity*. Retrieved from The American Presidency Project, http://www.presidency.ucsb.edu/ws/?pid=27448.

Lange, C., Rhim, L. M., & Ahearn, E. (2008). Special education in charter schools: The view from state education agencies. *Journal of Special Education Leadership*, *21*(1), 12–21.

Martin, C. C., and Hauth, C. (2015). *The survival guide for new special education teachers*. Arlington, VA: Council for Exceptional Children.

Mazzotti, V., & Rowe, D. (2015). *Building alliances: A how-to manual to support transitioning youth*. Arlington, VA: Council for Exceptional Children.

McCarney, S. B., Wunderlich, K. C., & House, S. N. (2014). *Pre-referral intervention manual* (4th ed.). Columbia, MO: Hawthorne Educational Services.

McKinney, J. R. (1996). Charter schools: A new barrier for children with disabilities. *Educational Leadership*, *54*(2), 22–25.

National Alliance for Public Charter Schools. (2009, June). *A new model law for supporting the growth of high-quality public charter schools*. Retrieved from http://www.publiccharters.org/wp-content/uploads/2014/01/ModelLaw_P7-wCVR_20110402T222341.pdf

National Alliance for Public Charter Schools. (2015a). *2014 annual report.* Retrieved from http://www.publiccharters.org/publications/2014-annual-report/

National Alliance for Public Charter Schools. (2015b). *Estimated number of public charter schools and students, 2014-2015.* Washington, DC: Author. Retrieved from http://www.publiccharters.org/wp-content/uploads/2015/02/open_closed_FINAL.pdf

National Association of Charter School Authorizers. (2015a). *Principals & standards for quality charter school authorizing.* Chicago, IL: Author. Retrieved from http://www.qualitycharters.org/for-authorizers/principles-and-standards/

National Association of Charter School Authorizers. (2015b). *State of charter authorizing 2015 report.* Chicago, IL: Author. Retrieved from http://www.qualitycharters.org/research-policies/archive/state-of-charter-authorizing-2015/

National Charter School Resource Center, American Institutes of Research. (2012). *Special education start-up and implementation tools for charter school leaders and special education managers.* Washington, DC: Author. Retrieved from https://www.charterschoolcenter.org/sites/default/files/files/field_publication_attachment/2114%20Start-Up%20Guide%20WEB%20d1_0_0.pdf

National Commission on Excellence in Education. (1983). *A nation at risk: The imperative for educational reform.* Washington, DC: U.S. Department of Education. Retrieved from http://www2.ed.gov/pubs/NatAtRisk/index.html

No Child Left Behind Act of 2001, 20 U.S.C. §§ 6301 et seq. (2006 & Supp. V. 2011)

Noonan, P. (2014). *Transition teaming: Twenty-six strategies for interagency collaboration.* Arlington, VA: Council for Exceptional Children.

Rehabilitation Act of 1973, 29 U.S.C. § 701 *et seq.* (2006).

Rhim, L. M., Ahearn, E., & Lange, C. (2007). Considering legal identity as a critical variable of interest in charter schools research. *Journal of School Choice 1,* 115–122. doi:10.1300/J467v01n03_11

Rhim, L. M., Ahearn, E. M., Lange, C. M., & McLaughlin, M. J. (2003) Balancing disparate visions—An analysis of special education in charter schools. In K. Bulkley & P. Wohlstetter, (Eds.), *Taking account of charter schools: What's happened and what's next?* (pp. 142–160). New York, NY: Teachers College Press.

Rhim, L. M., & Brinson, D. (2010). *Retrofitting bureaucracy: Factors influencing charter schools' access to federal entitlement programs.* Lincoln, IL: Center on Innovation and Improvement. Retrieved from http://www.adi.org/about/downloads/Retrofitting_Bureaucracy.pdf

Rhim, L. M., Gumz, J., & Henderson, K. (2015). *Key trends in special education in charter schools: Secondary analysis of the civil rights data collection 2011–2012.* New York, NY: National Center for Special Education in Charter Schools.

Rhim, L. M., & O'Neill, P. T. (2012). *Charter school authorizer rubrics for assessing special education capacity.* Washington, DC: National Charter School Resource Center, American Institutes of Research. http://www.qualitycharters.org/wp-content/uploads/2015/10/SchoolsForAll_Rubric-LEAs_Handout.pdf

Rhim, L. M., & O'Neill, P. T. (2013). *Improving access and creating exceptional opportunities for students with disabilities in public charter schools.* Washington, DC: National Alliance for Public Charter Schools. Retrieved from http://www.publiccharters.org/publications/improving-access-creating-exceptional-opportunities-students-disabilities-public-charter-schools/

Samuels, C. (2016, April 19). Number of U.S. students in special education ticks upward. *Education Week.* Retrieved from http://www.edweek.org/ew/articles/2016/04/20/number-of-us-students-in-special-education.html?cmp=SOC-SHR-TW

Section 504 of the Rehabilitation Act of 1973, as amended 29 U.S.C. § 794.

Shanker, A. (1988, March 31). *National Press Club speech. Albert Shanker, President, American Federation of Teachers.* Washington, DC: National Press Club. Retrieved from https://reuther.wayne.edu/files/64.43.pdf

Shaw, M. (2011, May). *Navigating the closure process.* (Authorizing Matters Issue Brief). Chicago, IL: NACSA. Retrieved from http://www.qualitycharters.org/wp-content/uploads/2015/11/Issue-Brief_NavigatingTheClosureProcess_2011.05.pdf

Sopko, K. M. (2008, March). *Summary of performance.* Washington, DC: National Association of State Directors of Special Education.. Retrieved from http://www.nasdse.org/Portals/0/SummaryofPerformance.pdf

U.S. Department of Education. (2014). *Thirty-sixth annual report to Congress on the implementation of the Individuals With Disabilities Education Act.* Washington, DC: Author. Retrieved from http://www2.ed.gov/about/reports/annual/osep/2014/parts-b-c/36th-idea-arc.pdf

U.S Department of Education. (2015). *Notice of final priorities, requirements, definitions, and selection criteria; Charter schools program grants to state educational agencies* (80 FR 34201). Retrieved from http://www2.ed.gov/programs/charter/legislation.html

U.S. Department of Justice. (2010). *ADA standards for accessible design.* Washington, DC: Author. Retrieved from http://www.ada.gov/2010ADAstandards_index.htm

Vaughn G. et al., v. the Mayor and City Council of Baltimore Civ. Action No. MJG-84-1911 (2004).

Vaughn, S., & Swanson, E. A. (2015). Special education research advances knowledge in education. *Exceptional Children, 82*, 11–24. doi:10.1177/0014402915598781

Vergari, S. (2000). The regulatory styles of statewide charter school authorizers: Arizona, Massachusetts, and Michigan. *Education Administration Quarterly, 36*, 730-757.

Wechtenhiser, K., Wade, A., & Lin, M. (Eds.) (2010). *Accountability in action: A comprehensive guide to charter school closure.* Chicago, IL: NACSA. Retrieved from https://www.charterschoolcenter.org/resource/accountability-action-comprehensive-guide-charter-school-closure

Wolf, P. J. (2012). *The comprehensive longitudinal evaluation of the Milwaukee Parental Choice Program: Summary of the final reports.* Fayetteville, AR: Department of Education Reform, School Choice Demonstration Project, University of Arkansas. Retrieved from http://www.uaedreform.org/downloads/2012/02/report-36-the-comprehensive-longitudinal-evaluation-of-the-milwaukee-parental-choice-program.pdf

Woolley, J., & Peters, G. (1999-2016). Lyndon B. Johnson: "Special Message to the Congress: Toward Full Educational Opportunity," January 12, 1965. The American Presidency Project, University of California, Santa Barbara. Retrieved from http://www.presidency.ucsb.edu/ws/?pid=27448

Wright, P., & Wright, P. (2007a). The Child Find mandate: What does it mean to you? *Wrightslaw.* Retrieved from http://www.wrightslaw.com/info/child.find.mandate.htm

Wright, P. W. D., & Wright, P. D. (2007b). *Wrightslaw: Special education law* (2nd ed.). Deltaville, VA: Harbor House Law Press.

Wrightslaw. (2010, March). *Transition: Summary of performance (SOP).* Retrieved from http://www.wrightslaw.com/info/trans.sop.template.pdf

Best Practices in Special Education for Charter Schools

AREA OR SERVICE	KEY CONSIDERATIONS	BEST PRACTICES
Child Find and enrollment	• How will the school identify students who may benefit from special education evaluations? • How will the school make the local community aware that the school is inclusive, and can screen students for eligibility to receive special education and related services and thereafter provide these services? • Does the school plan to employ a staff member who is knowledgeable about the Child Find requirement? If not, how will the staff receive access to special education information and guidance?	• Child Find is not a single action but rather an ongoing process to raise community awareness about available screening, assessment, and service provision. Charter schools must have a process to inform the community, as well as parents of enrolled students, about the availability of evaluative screenings for special education and related services. • The process typically entails advertising screening services to the general public as part of student recruitment activities as well as promoting awareness of screening and services for students already enrolled. • Schools are responsible for identifying any student who is enrolled in the school who is presenting academic or behavioral problems and determining whether that child should be referred for a special education evaluation. • Special education should be an integral part of all recruitment activities and materials. To make certain that the school is an attractive option for all students, the school's marketing, application, and enrollment materials and procedures may not discourage applications from students with disabilities. Having a disability is not an acceptable reason to deny admission, and would constitute discrimination specifically banned by federal law.

AREA OR SERVICE	KEY CONSIDERATIONS	BEST PRACTICES
Staffing	• How will special education staff collaborate with general education teachers and administrators (e.g., co-teaching, collaborative planning)? • If there is a shortage of special education teachers in the community, what creative solutions can the school practice to employ more (e.g., offer teachers support or incentives to become dual certified, investigate sharing staff with other schools)? • What administrator will be designated as the "point person" to liaise with families receiving evaluations and special education services? • If the school contracts with an external provider for special education and related services, how will these services be coordinated?	• Schools should anticipate that at least 10% to 12% of their student population will require special education services. • Charter schools should ensure that they adhere to federal and state laws when employing staff or contracting with others to provide services to students with disabilities (i.e., Americans With Disabilities Act, Individuals With Disabilities Education Act, Section 504 of the Rehabilitation Act of 1973). • Special education services involve general education teachers as well as special education teachers and related service providers. Charter schools should strive to hire and retain high-quality instructional personnel who believe that all students can learn and who also support the charter school's mission.
Facility	• Is the school's physical building accessible to individuals with disabilities? • Does the school's facility include space to provide support services outside of the general education classroom, when needed? • Does the school have access to storage space to house student records in accordance with federal privacy requirements?	• Charter school facilities must be consistent with local and state health and safety requirements as well as with the federal Americans With Disabilities Act and Section 504 of the Rehabilitation Act of 1973. Accessibility measures should be in place when the school opens, in anticipation of a student or parent having a disability, as opposed to retrofitting an inaccessible structure when needed. • An inaccessible building is a potential deterrent that may limit the number of students with disabilities who enroll in the school. Building renovations must comply with applicable rules and could trigger additional responsibilities related to access.

AREA OR SERVICE	KEY CONSIDERATIONS	BEST PRACTICES
Funding	• How will federal, state, and local special education dollars flow to benefit students with disabilities enrolled in the charter school? • How will those dollars and their expenditure be tracked? • Is the school eligible to receive Medicaid reimbursements?	• Both the authorizer and the charter school should have a clear understanding of how dollars, or services purchased with funds allocated to special education, will flow to the school. Lack of transparency or overcomplicated funding procedures can lead to mistrust and incorrect assumptions about the extent to which charter schools are receiving their funding.
Curriculum and instruction	• How will the school modify delivery of curriculum (e.g., using assistive technology, universal design for learning, etc.) to ensure that all students can access the general education curriculum? • How does the school plan to train teachers to modify the curriculum and instruction to address the unique needs of students with disabilities? • How will curriculum and instruction decisions be tracked and monitored by IEP teams and other school personnel?	• Supporting students' access to the general education curriculum is the purpose of providing special education and related services. Charter schools should have a clear plan to ensure that all students can access the curriculum and that instructional techniques will be adapted to serve all students.
Assessment	• How will the school identify students who may be struggling and would benefit from academic interventions? • How will the school implement evidence-based early interventions (i.e., response to intervention) and track student progress? • How will the school identify appropriate accommodations for students with disabilities taking assessments?	• Assessments must incorporate the same supports and accommodations that students with disabilities receive in the classroom. Charter schools also should identify alternate metrics to evaluate the progress of students with disabilities (e.g., progress toward meeting goals outlined in IEPs, amount of time in general education classrooms, success after matriculation).
IEP development	• What are the school's procedures for communicating with parents about their and their children's IDEA rights? • What is the school's plan for scheduling, leading, and documenting IEP meetings? • If the school is a middle school or high school, does it have an understanding of and the ability to develop appropriate transition plans in accordance with IDEA regulations?	• The IEP is an evolving document that reflects the unique needs of a student with disabilities and the individual services to be provided to enable them to access the general education curriculum and succeed at school. Developing an IEP requires a significant level of knowledge of IDEA as well as state special education rules and regulations. Charter schools should be able to articulate a clear and feasible plan for how IEPs will be developed.

Area or service	Key considerations	Best practices
Progress monitoring	● How will the school track progress of students with disabilities aside from standardized state tests (e.g., progress on IEP goals, degree of inclusion in the general education classroom, student retention and graduation, postgraduation opportunities)?	● Annual standardized assessment are a relatively blunt instrument used to track student progress. Charter schools have the ability to identify a variety of measures to track the academic progress of students with disabilities that are more nuanced than annual tests and more substantive than review of inputs (e.g., complete and up-to-date IEPs and compliance with IEPs).
Discipline	● What is the school's discipline policy, and does it address the needs of students with disabilities (e.g., students with behavioral disorders)? ● If adopting an existing district's discipline policy, do school personnel fully understand the nuances of the policy as applied in a charter setting and as applied to students with disabilities? ● How will the school train all personnel regarding the discipline policy, a schoolwide positive behavior plan, and the nuances involved in disciplining students with disabilities? ● How will the school manage manifestation determination hearings, if it as an LEA is required to convene them?	● Charter schools should have thoughtful and fair discipline policies that reflect the school's educational philosophy and best instructional practices. These policies should be consistent with applicable laws and regulations relating to disciplining students with disabilities. The goal of discipline is to teach children how to behave and provide a safe environment in which all students can succeed absent distractions. ● It is important that at least one staff member fully understand the specific requirements of IDEA and its regulations for applying discipline to students with disabilities. Schools should clearly articulate behavior expectations and consequences.
Compliance	● How does the charter school maintain special education records that comply with state and federal rules and regulations? ● How will the school document and resolve complaints related to educating students with disabilities? ● What is the school's plan for mediating disputes relating to services for students with disabilities, to avoid due process litigation?	● Special education is highly regulated, and, consequently, compliance with federal and state regulations is a part of developing and sustaining a high-quality special education program. Charter schools must follow procedural as well as more substantive programmatic requirements to comply with the spirit as well as the letter of the law.

Area or service	Key considerations	Best practices
		• Central to compliance is ensuring that students with disabilities are provided a free appropriate public education in the least restrictive environment. Underlying these central tenets of special education are policies and procedures related to informing parents of their rights and ensuring that students are provided with timely assessments and regular monitoring of their progress toward achieving the goals outlined in their IEPs Section 504 plans. • School leaders should strive to establish highly transparent policies and procedures and engage parents to the maximum extent possible. By recognizing and engaging parents as essential partners in their child's education, school leaders can minimize and defuse problems that may arise. There should be evidence of a commitment to involving parents in clear and regular communication about services.

Note. Adapted with permission from *Charter School Authorizer Rubrics for Assessing Special Education Capacity,* by L. M. Rhim and P. T. O'Neill, pp. 3–18. Copyright 2012 by the National Charter School Resource Center, American Institutes of Research.

Glossary of Special Education Acronyms

ABA	Applied behavior analysis		LEA	Local education agency
ADA	Americans With Disabilities Act		LRE	Least restrictive environment
ADHD	Attention deficit hyperactivity disorder		NCLB	No Child Left Behind Act of 2001
ASD	Autism spectrum disorder		OCD	Obsessive compulsive disorder
ASVAB	Armed Services Vocational Aptitude Battery Test		OHI	Other health impairment
AT	Assistive technology		OSEP	U.S. Department of Education Office of Special Education Programs
BIP	Behavior intervention plan		OT	Occupational therapy
BYOD	Bring your own device		PARCC	Partnership for Assessment of Readiness for College and Careers
CBM	Curriculum-based measurement		PBIS	Positive behavior interventions and supports
CCSS	Common Core State Standards			
CFR	U.S. Code of Federal Regulations		PDD	Pervasive developmental disorder
CLD	Culturally and linguistically diverse		PLAAFP	Present level of academic achievement and functional performance
DD	Developmental delay			
DSM	Diagnostic and Statistical Manual of Mental Disorders		PLC	Professional learning communities
			PLOP	Present level of performance
EBP	Evidence-based practice		PT	Physical therapy
ECE	Early childhood education		RC	Responsive Classroom
ED	Emotional disability (or disorder)		RTI	Response to intervention
ED	U.S. Department of Education		SWPBIS	Schoolwide positive behavior interventions and supports
ELL	English language learner			
ESY	Extended school year		SBAC	Smarter Balanced Assessment Consortium
FAPE	Free and appropriate education		SEA	State education agency
FBA	Functional behavior assessment		SEAC	Special education advisory team
FERPA	Family Educational Rights and Privacy Act		SLD	Specific learning disability
IDEA	Individuals With Disabilities Education Act		SRSD	Self-regulated strategy development
IEE	Independent educational evaluation		SWD	Students with disabilities
IEP	Individualized education program		TBI	Traumatic brain injury
IT	Instructional technology		UDL	Universal design for learning
LD	Learning disability			

Note. Adapted from *The Survival Guide for New Special Education Teachers,* by C. Creighton Martin and C. Hauth, pp. 141–142. Copyright 2015 Council for Exceptional Children.

Disciplinary Procedures
for Students With Disabilities

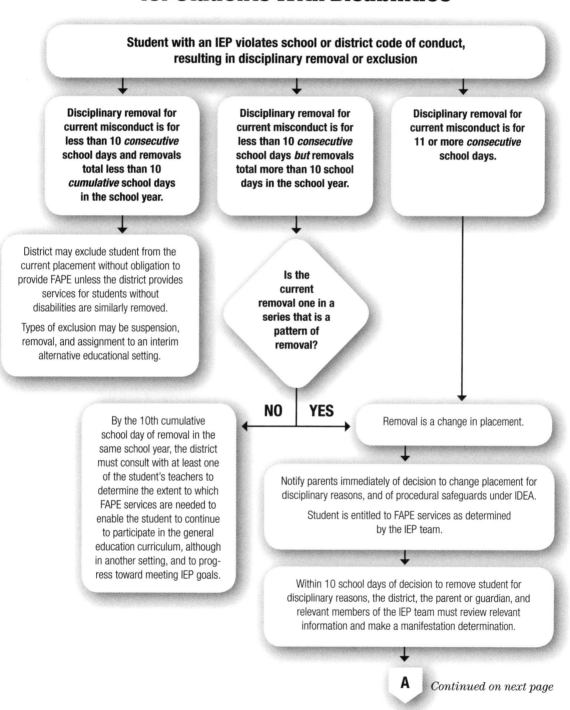

Student with an IEP violates school or district code of conduct, resulting in disciplinary removal or exclusion

Disciplinary removal for current misconduct is for less than 10 *consecutive* school days and removals total less than 10 *cumulative* school days in the school year.

Disciplinary removal for current misconduct is for less than 10 *consecutive* school days *but* removals total more than 10 school days in the school year.

Disciplinary removal for current misconduct is for 11 or more *consecutive* school days.

District may exclude student from the current placement without obligation to provide FAPE unless the district provides services for students without disabilities are similarly removed.

Types of exclusion may be suspension, removal, and assignment to an interim alternative educational setting.

Is the current removal one in a series that is a pattern of removal?

By the 10th cumulative school day of removal in the same school year, the district must consult with at least one of the student's teachers to determine the extent to which FAPE services are needed to enable the student to continue to participate in the general education curriculum, although in another setting, and to progress toward meeting IEP goals.

NO | **YES**

Removal is a change in placement.

Notify parents immediately of decision to change placement for disciplinary reasons, and of procedural safeguards under IDEA.

Student is entitled to FAPE services as determined by the IEP team.

Within 10 school days of decision to remove student for disciplinary reasons, the district, the parent or guardian, and relevant members of the IEP team must review relevant information and make a manifestation determination.

A *Continued on next page*

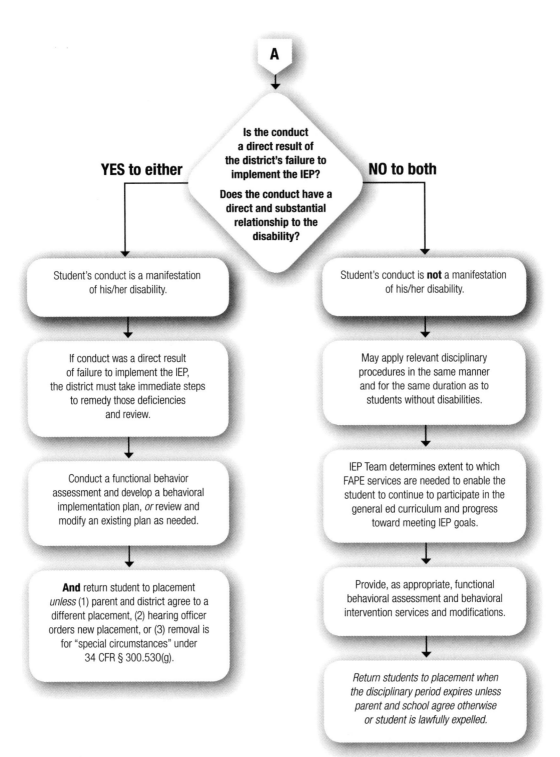

A

Is the conduct a direct result of the district's failure to implement the IEP?

Does the conduct have a direct and substantial relationship to the disability?

YES to either

NO to both

Student's conduct is a manifestation of his/her disability.

Student's conduct is **not** a manifestation of his/her disability.

If conduct was a direct result of failure to implement the IEP, the district must take immediate steps to remedy those deficiencies and review.

May apply relevant disciplinary procedures in the same manner and for the same duration as to students without disabilities.

Conduct a functional behavior assessment and develop a behavioral implementation plan, *or* review and modify an existing plan as needed.

IEP Team determines extent to which FAPE services are needed to enable the student to continue to participate in the general ed curriculum and progress toward meeting IEP goals.

And return student to placement *unless* (1) parent and district agree to a different placement, (2) hearing officer orders new placement, or (3) removal is for "special circumstances" under 34 CFR § 300.530(g).

Provide, as appropriate, functional behavioral assessment and behavioral intervention services and modifications.

Return students to placement when the disciplinary period expires unless parent and school agree otherwise or student is lawfully expelled.

Index